SPIRITUAL LIFE SAVERS

Smooth Sailing for the Soul

SPIRITUAL LIFE SAVERS

Smooth Sailing for the Soul

Gloria D. Benish

CITADEL PRESS
Kensington Publishing Corp.
www.kensingtonbooks.com

CITADEL PRESS BOOKS are published by

Kensington Publishing Corp.
850 Third Avenue
New York, NY 10022

All Kensington titles, imprints, and distributed lines are available at special quantity discounts for bulk purchases for sales promotions, premiums, fund-raising, educational, or institutional use. Special book excerpts or customized printings can also be created to fit specific needs. For details, write or phone the office of the Kensington special sales manager: Kensington Publishing Corp., 850 Third Avenue, New York, NY 10022, attn: Special Sales Department, phone 1-800-221-2647.

First printing: May 2002

10 9 8 7 6 5 4 3 2 1

Printed in the United States of America

Library of Congress Control Number: 2001099797

ISBN: 0-8065-2263-1

To MY HUSBAND, KIRK,

LISTEN TO MY HEART . . .

I've loved a lot of men in my life and could have made do,
But true love found me the day I laid eyes upon you.
There's many a sad story, loving the wrong man 'n lessons
    learned,
But we're taught if you play with fire, you're gonna get burned.

It's true, I got consumed from falling in love with you,
And all of my senses tell me that you can feel it, too.
In our passion, I only have eyes for you, 'n you for me,
And that's the way it is . . . the way it needs to be.

Lay your head upon my breast and listen to my heart,
Cities, nor walls of flesh, can ever keep us apart.
My heart never lies, my love, it's the song of my soul,
You're the only man for me, the one who makes me whole.

I can see your love returned, in the light of your eyes,
The scent of purity, around us, also testifies.
I got burned from loving you, there's no need to blame,
Alone, we were a single match, and together, an eternal flame.

Lay your head upon my breast and listen to my heart,
Cities, nor walls of flesh, can ever keep us apart.
My heart never lies, my love, it's the song of my soul,
You're the only man for me, the one who makes me whole.

I got burned from loving you, there's no need to blame,
Alone, we were a single match, and together, an eternal flame.

Always,
Gloria

Contents

Part Two
LEARNING HOW TO SURRENDER JUDGMENT

Part Three
DON'T TAKE IT PERSONALLY

Acknowledgments

Walter Zacharius: To give credit, where credit is due, the world should know that it all began with you. Countless publishers reviewed my books; one even said, "If I don't offer you a two- or three-book contract, it's going to be the biggest mistake I ever made." You saw something beyond *just publishing a book—you listened to your heart*, and I'll make you proud. Count on it. Thank you for taking a risk with a "first-time author."

Ann LaFarge: I appreciate your expertise at editing, being a loyal long-time member of the Kensington/Citadel family. Joining talents, I realized immediately that your abilities as an "architect" ensured that my idea would be built upon a solid foundation. Your planning helped me to structure a timeless and ageless path for others. Thank you.

Linda K. (Nikki) Fudge: For being my inspiration to take the reader on a promotional trip like we went on, countless times, together. Unlike our trips out, I allowed this copilot the opportunity to talk, too. See chapter 20, and smile . . . You are the best friend I could ever have. I love you, Linda Kay Fudge.

My children: **Kerrie, Jaime, D.W.,** and **Danielle**—you make me so proud. You make writing books about our family so easy.

My "keeper" sons-in-law: **Christopher** and **Keith**—thanks for making my daughters so happy.

My grandson, **Colton:** "Colton Lee rhymes with apple tree," a reminder of the bazillions of hours we spent together, swinging, at the park. I love riding bikes with you, roller skating, playing the pinball machine, reading one book after another, flying our kite, running in three-legged races together, and having late-night talks in bed while we hold hands and do "love light." I love being four years old with you. I like being your granny.

My parents, **Allen** and **Esther Hale:** You've said you wanted to live long enough to see everything I've ever attempted to accomplish become reality. Me, too. Who would have ever thought that "overnight success takes fifteen (or more) years?" Thank you for supporting me, listening to years of my goals, and encouraging me when I felt discouraged. I love you, Dad and Mom.

My "adopted" parents, **Fred** and **Dorothy:** I daily hold you in my heart and thoughts. Our love was made in heaven, and on earth, we met again. And people ask me if I've ever seen an angel? Yes, and with no doubt, I've had the pleasure of two earth angels . . . but where do you two hide your wings when others are looking?

To the Reader:
Modern-Day Prodigal Son

I whisper to you in the wind, through the tall pines, beckoning you to return home to the safety of My arms. I did not ask you to leave the security of My heart to venture off into a drama of fears, but, because I loved you and you chose to explore and create, I allowed you to go. I trust enough in your love for Me, that when you are bone-tired of the trials and tribulations that the glamour of the world has to offer . . . you will call out My name and I will tenderly fill you with My peace.

I believe it's only pride that keeps you from surrendering your fears and judgments, allowing My greater power to direct your life. When you are ready, I am here.

You may not see, hear, or feel Me, but I am with you always. When you choose no longer to experience pain and sadness, come home.

I beg you nightly in your dreams to come back to Me so I can give you the world, but My cries go unheeded because you believe the magic of the world has more to offer than I do.

Everything I created returns to Me sooner or later, and I would like your journey into love to be today, this moment . . . accepting that I, Who created you, know better than anyone else what is best for you.

You say you love Me, with your heart, mind, and soul—but will you allow Me to fill you with love, wisdom, direction, and guidance? You fear Me, for ancestors have taught you of judgment and ignorance, but in reality, I am softer than a summer rain and more loving, patient, and kind than the greatest saint.

Always and all ways, I want you to know that no matter what you choose, you shall have My unconditional love, acceptance, pride, and support. I offer you rest if you are weary . . . you can live in My mansion and wear the Robe of Christ (Consciousness), experiencing the greatest pleasures of My Kingdom.

Know Me, love Me . . . but child, return to Me—for, I, your Creator, bless you with All That I Am . . .

Your Heavenly Father

Introduction

My husband, Kirk, and I just returned from a ten-year anniversary celebration on the Oregon coast. I think it's ironic that we would choose a vacation at the sea, just before I began writing a book with this title. Weather reports forewarned of rain during our entire visit, but having no expectations or plans, other than being together, nothing could threaten our time alone.

As promised, when we reached our rented condo on the beach, there was a thunderstorm, and I watched from our room as the waves crashed against the rocks and the shore. They appeared angry and aggressive. The driving rain and the waves were beautiful.

I thought, "How like life these waves are. Just when we seem to have smooth sailing and everything is going right, we find ourselves getting hit hard with a turn of life's events." For me, incorporating spirituality into every moment of my life is ordinary and completely spontaneous. Miracles and meatloaf.

To do so, I realized that three spiritual life-saving tips keep me in the natural flow of love and peace. I don't want to cloud your perception of what you, personally, need to draw from this book that can bring you this same reality, so I won't focus full attention on just three spiritual tips. You may find that one sentence transforms your life and answers a long-held question. Or, you may find an entire life makeover by incorporating everything you read.

Spiritual growth is an individual process. My "voice" is but one of many. My previous editor phoned me one afternoon and mentioned a title that is available to readers and he moaned, "Gloria, I wish that was the title for one of your books. It's so perfect for who you are and what you do." He feared we had "missed" an opportunity by not having that title for my own.

"Sir, I don't need that title. I'm not in competition with anyone (as there is NO competition in Spirit). No one has my individual personality, writing style, or miracle stories."

He, of course, agreed. My writings will touch those who are drawn to be touched.

With this book in your hand, you're invited into my world. I will be using examples and experiences that touch my life. They may be the same exact issues you're dealing with, or different ones. If you can see how I relate to them in a spiritual manner, you will have the ability to resolve them in your life.

Through the following stories and anecdotes, I invite you to join me on a journey. You can learn these and other life-saving tips. In my book, *Go Within or Go Without,* I opened my heart and home to you. As you stepped over the threshold, you sat at my kitchen table and experienced a day with me. For this book, I'd like to ask you to join me, in spirit, on a two-day promotional road trip to Spokane, Washington, where I'm being asked to be an inspirational speaker for two evenings.

This "trip" will allow us quality time with one another. I will be able to give you undivided, uninterrupted time as we share our lives and this experience. You'll give me an opportunity and outlet to speak of the things that I don't normally have time (or courage) to discuss publicly.

This vacation is one you can afford to take—**all your needs will be met.** If you have any worries or fears, bring them along for the ride so we can discuss them. If you've only been on "guilt trips" lately (or forever), this is an opportunity to make yourself the priority for a change. This time is just for YOU. You are going to have the time of your life. We'll laugh, and perhaps even cry with one another.

So, pack your spiritual bags and come along with me. It will be a journey you'll remember for the rest of your life . . .

Always,
Gloria D. Benish
(Alias: Dr. Glo-bug—just here "to lighten things up")

Part One

UNDERSTANDING ONENESS

1
Bridge Over
Troubled Minds

Your timing is perfect. I had just knelt on the sofa and raised my pinkie, index finger and thumb, in the universal sign language position of "I love you," as my husband, Kirk, drove away. How nice that you would drive up and see my hand in that position, as well. Welcome to my world.

Give me a hug and don't let go until I tell you. I'm placing my right palm on the lower part of your head, supporting you as if you're a newborn. My left arm enfolds you and draws you near to my heart.

Close your eyes and imagine we are long-lost friends, reunited once again. My left, open palm is softly massaging and affectionately stroking your back, floating lightly up and down your spine. As we hug, I'm erasing your aches, pains, and heartaches, and removing the burdens you've carried, alone, for such a long time.

In my arms, and close to my chest, you feel the warmth, comfort, security, and love as my heart center opens to the size of the Grand Canyon. You can feel the genuine concern and compassion. You can feel that who you were, or anything you've done, past this moment in time, doesn't matter to me. All that matters is this moment of who you are right now.

You can feel an icy/hot, pure engulfing cape of the most extraordinary love you'd never known was possible. I whisper one simple, but profoundly truthful statement as we embrace: "Take all you want . . . there's plenty for everyone."

How is it that two strangers are uniting and feeling like we've known each other forever? How can it be, that though we've just met, we don't want to release one another from the embrace?

We're told that love is the glue that holds our universe together, but from a human standpoint, we might think that even if this is true, our world seems to be falling apart.

Divine Love reunites us as One and we remember it once it is felt. Divine Love, which has no conditions, expectations, or judgments on it, **is** the glue that holds us together.

Before we part from the hug, I softly whisper in your ear, "I love you with my *whole,* great big heart . . . and I ain't kidding either."

I'm so excited to take this journey with you. I'm grateful you would accept my invitation.

I just need to grab my luggage and I'll be ready to go. I already gassed the van and loaded my books and promotional flyers last night. I have also packed us a snack and some drinks, but I'm sure we'll stop for rest (or smoking) breaks along the way. Also, please feel safe enough to let me know your needs while we're together on this journey.

While you're putting your luggage into my minivan, I'm going to make one last trip through the house to make sure I turned off the coffeepot, locked the doors, and to "tinkle" one last time. If you want to finish your cigarette, or use the bathroom before we head out, I'll be ready in just a few minutes.

Gloria, I just noticed your license plate. I think it's cute that you have a personalized message of being a miracle worker.

Ha. I'm so glad you have a miracle state of consciousness. So many people noticed the initials M R C L W K R and asked me why I had "Mr. Clawalker" on my license plate. I had license holders made that endorsed "Miracle Healing Ministry" and my "Miracle Publishing Company," thinking the words would raise peoples' awareness of a miracle consciousness. Still, some people only read it as Mr. Clawalker. It certainly proves that life, in this world, is a perception of our individual states of consciousness.

I can hardly wait to have this time with you, Gloria. I loved reading and hearing about your miracle-working adventures, and I'm excited to learn as much as I can while we're together.

I love sharing and am willing to teach every single person in this world as much as I can to have them experience a rich and fulfilling life. I've always teased that I have so much to say if someone will just listen. As you will discover if you haven't already, I'm able to talk about love and life IN SO MANY WORDS.

Also, I'd certainly like to make you aware that anything I share isn't done to impress you with my individual life and gifts. The stories and teachings are merely a reminder to awaken to your own gifts and talents. All these and greater experiences, in your day-to-day physical reality, are your birthright as well.

On your mark, get set, I'm READY TO GO. I already feel comfortable around you. I'm sure everyone says that, though. Before you even hugged me, I felt as if I'd known you forever.

Thank you. When my friend Nikki was my copilot for adventures like this, I learned and experienced what a friend is. We were able to be honest with each other and say whatever it was that we were thinking and feeling. I trust you and I will have that same opportunity while we're together.

Buckle your seatbelt, please. Even though we believe "God is our protection," we still live in a physical world and must take precautions. Every day of our life mirrors our present state of awareness. As we continue to grow spiritually, simple affirmations and newly established beliefs become our physical experience. Until we reach that level, however, we must not falsely assume that our words or present understanding will provide a perfect world unless we have healed our fears and dissolved our imperfect thinking.

I think the reason that people feel as if they "know" me is because they're remembering the Presence of Love. Also, so many people have said that the teaching I've brought to such a simple level has easily connected them to their spiritual Source. I love being a bridge between God and humanity. During the past sixteen years, I've listened to countless people with troubled minds. I am a third-generation motormouth, but I am a good listener too. During this trip, I have so much to learn from you, as well. I promise I'm going to let you talk also.

What a beautiful day for our trip. Four wonderful, leisurely hours of uninterrupted chat time on the drive to Spokane. There are many bridges to cross in your journey before you realize you didn't have to cross any to have a direct and personal connection to God.

2
How to Be
a Happy Hummer

Gloria, I've noticed that in just this short amount of time we've been together, I feel a warm and glowing sense in my body. I feel like a child again, without a care in the world. I'm not normally the type of person who would act silly, but I feel so playful around you. Maybe it's your smile or the love I feel while we're together. I trust you already and feel safe to be myself. Without a logical reason, I feel happy and content.

You're so complimentary! Thank you, again. The glowing sensation you're feeling is the Presence of God, not the presence of Gloria as the individual personality. I have that feeling off and on, throughout the day, as people are touching my consciousness and being healed. The childlike quality comes with the territory of experiencing that Presence.

Your mentioning how happy you feel reminds me of a recent experience. My sister-in-law, Debbie, had been scolding me constantly since she learned that I'd only had one Pap smear and one mammogram in the past decade. I made an appointment for my female 50,000-mile, ten-year checkup.

As I was lying in the uncompromising position (that I hope you're not visualizing about now), the doctor continued to ask me question after question about my health. To each concern of hers, I would reply repeatedly, "No, nope, nada, nothing, no to that also." Attempting to save her (and me) time, I said, "You can stop asking me those questions because there is absolutely nothing wrong with me."

She asked, "Do you mean to tell me that nothing peculiar is going on in your life?"

"Well, now that you mention it, there is one thing," I responded. "I'm so dang happy all the time, I can hardly stand myself." I continued by emphasizing the seriousness of the situation, "I hum all day long. Even in the middle of the night when I get up to tinkle, I have to make a conscious effort *not to hum* on the way back to bed."

Tickled, she replied, "If you're so happy then, you won't mind if I do the anal check," and I barked, "I'm not THAT damned happy."

Day in and day out, I'm a happy hummer. No one can rain on my parade. I have high energy, my life flows, and I absolutely love my life as I watch miracles occur on a daily basis.

The joy, love, and peace that you will learn to experience is an effect of opening yourself to the Presence of God. Since I became conscious of that Presence, I have witnessed thousands of miracles. As you become aware, you will watch, as your life becomes easier without human effort. As you practice those tips I teach, you will begin experiencing confidence, courage, strength, and the attributes you've always admired in others. You'll see how simple this all can be.

Gloria, I now understand why you have nicknamed yourself *Dr. Glo-bug.* You have such a lighthearted, playful spirit, and you can take the most mundane experience and make it almost comical. You're good at "lightening things up." I already feel lighter and can almost believe that I, too, could know my purpose in this life.

It was nearly a year ago that I realized I was reaching lifelong goals. Through an instantaneous knowingness, a one-liner had filled my thoughts one morning. I began pondering the inner guidance and watched *immediate* results. I shared the guidance with those who called from across the miles for healing, inspiration, and friendship.

CONCERNING (FILL IN THE BLANK WITH YOUR OWN CONCERN), I UNIFY MY DREAMS, DESIRES, PURPOSE, AND WILL WITH GOD

I had struggled for years to find a publisher. I repeated the above, "Concerning my books, I unify my dreams, desires, purpose, and Will with God." A New York publisher contacted me and offered me a four-book contract, with a five-book option. I was told that it was virtually unheard of, in the publishing industry, for a first-time author to receive such a deal.

Also, five years ago, I wrote a love song for my husband, Kirk. I silently pondered, "Concerning this love song, I unify my dreams, desires, purpose, and Will with God." A Nashville music publisher contacted me within days and signed a contract with me to record "Throughout Eternity."

I shared the one-liner with my local spiritual group and several members spoke of their immediate results at the following meetings.

We struggle, humanly (the hard way), to achieve everything we attempt to do. For me, personally, those years on the spiritual path gave me a deeper understanding of life and my beliefs, so the adversity served me well. Those struggles also gave me the ability to grow through them so that I could be a more effective spiritual teacher or leader.

However, reaching a spiritual level of understanding of why this simple, yet profound statement could affect the physical world dazzled even me.

So many that call upon me, as a spiritual adviser or teacher, would beg me to tell them their life's purpose. In a moment, you can know yours . . . by realizing your purpose is not separate from God's. You will learn, throughout our time together, that your purpose is just to be you.

As you awaken daily, unify your purpose with the Presence. Listen to your thoughts, take physical action when you can, and you will find that fun and exciting new experiences begin occurring for you. Again, your Divine Purpose is to be yourself. Your talents, creative ventures, or gifts are a result of following that Divine Plan made uniquely just for you.

Your desires aren't separate from His. Your Will is One with God. There aren't two Wills, His and yours. Your dreams are His dreams.

Concerning this trip of ours—and this book—I unify the desires, dreams, purpose, and Will with God. Everything that touches this experience, from beginning to end, is perfection made manifest.

How do you know when you've separated yourself from the Presence? Are you in love or are you in fear?

Dr. Glo-bug (if you don't really mind me calling you that), you make everything sound so simple . . . like we can all understand and experience the same miracles you

do every day of your life. How is it that we can overcome our fears as we become aware of them?

It's very interesting that the answer to that question was learned on this very road we're traveling upon. Many years ago, I was driving to Spokane to do private healings for three days. I spent two years of my service driving to Spokane, every other weekend, to make myself more available to those in need.

On that certain trip, it was the first time I didn't have a traveling companion along for the ride. I had never driven over the two mountain passes alone.

I felt fear. "What ifs" flooded my mind. What if I break down? I don't know how to change a flat tire. I don't have a cell phone. . . .

Because I felt fear, I knew I had separated myself from God. I silently pleaded, "God, I'm asking for a conscious realization of your Presence." An electric bolt of energy began down between my ankles and shivered itself up through my body.

"I'm not impressed," I silently replied. I was still feeling fear.

I stated a second, silent request. "God, I'm asking, again, for a conscious realization of your Presence." I felt the "rock 'em, sock 'em, knock you off your barstool" thunder of silence fill me, as I heard the voice of my soul reply, "I appear in many forms." However, along with the inner whisper, my intuition filled me with a direct knowingness, that the van surrounding me, the pavement beneath, the trees on the right, and the vehicles that passed me on the left were all God, but appearing in many forms.

Silently, I replied, "Now, I'm impressed." I was no longer feeling fear. I was back in love.

Daily, we separate people, places, and things from the One and Only Original Source. We call them names—Mary, Joe, and Joe's kid. We call them potatoes, cigarettes, alcohol, and roses. But, no matter what we name each person, place, or thing, they are all still God, but appearing in many forms.

It's good that we label people, pets, inanimate objects, and food as separate names, or things could get confusing. But God is all those things. God is (spiritual) good, which has no opposite. Seeking Oneness, in all things and in all ways, introduces you to the spiritual realm that doesn't fluctuate between the good and bad we have thus far experienced.

Realizing our Oneness with all spiritual good allows us to become a Happy Hummer, no longer riding the emotional roller coaster. Each time we listen to our heart we discover a greater sense of peace. Those of us who don't initially trust our heart, rationalizing our choices with our head, soon find—with practice—that our heart doesn't lie.

I'm not sure if I know how to listen to my heart. Can you explain how I might know for sure? Also, I'm still a people pleaser, wanting approval. I fear letting loved ones and friends down in their times of need. Do you have an example of what I might do when I find myself in that kind of situation?

You'll be lucky if I only offer one suggestion to your question. My biggest problem is to know when to shut up and not offer too many illustrations. (I'm working on that though. . . .)

To answer your need, however, one of my local spiritual group members called and asked if I would drive to a nearby town and heal her dying friend. My heart immediately said, "No." I apologized to Sandy, attempting to explain that my head and guilt said, "Yes," but I would have to get back to her.

My mind told me all the reasons I "should" agree. *I could be this woman's last chance. My God, Gloria, you've flown the friendly skies, from sea to shining sea, to assist other requests— are you really so busy that you can't drive twenty miles to help someone?* I felt so ashamed to have a beautiful gift and deny anyone.

I meditated several times and the answer continued to be "No." I took a late-night walk, seeking further guidance. My inner voice continued to urge me to say "No."

I awoke early the next morning and meditated a third time. (I thought I'd keep asking, "until He got it right".) I still felt uneasy about fulfilling the simple request. I asked myself countless times, "Are you thinking you should say 'yes' to be nice and receive approval? Are you seeking control?" Honestly, I didn't feel that I needed approval, nor control. My heart continued to say "no" although I didn't understand, humanly, why.

I telephoned my friend and apologized. "I don't understand why, Sandy, but I have to say 'No' to this request." She said she understood.

Days later, I received a call and Sandy explained that if I had driven to her friend's home on the requested day, I would have met severe opposition. The dying woman and her mother were having an argument. The trip would have wasted my time.

A week later, a second call came. I was asked again if I would offer a helping hand and my heart immediately responded happily with "Yes." The healing, however, resulted in the woman choosing to die. She asked for her fears of death to be dissolved so she could pass in peace. Had I responded to the first request, it would have been a waste of my time because the woman was still in confusion as to whether she wanted to stay or go.

Remember: I unify my gifts and talents with the dreams, desires, purpose, and Will of God.

When you realize a conscious Oneness, concerning each request of your day, every event and outcome is in Divine Order. You will no longer second-guess or assume how you think things should manifest. Allow Spirit to guide you.

There is only one mind, God consciousness, and being aware of this truth, you will watch as miracles unfold minute by minute. Remember neither you nor I see the Divine Plan. Good, however, stands behind all appearances.

God called.
You need to answer.
He speaks.
You must listen.
He guides.
You must take physical action.
Miracles happen.
It's that simple . . . to be a Happy Hummer, too.

I'm willing to walk each step of the way with you, throughout the remainder of this life, teaching as I learn, understand, and experience these spiritual truths as my reality. You, too, can and will understand how to blend spirituality into every day of your life.

3

One Person Can
Make a Difference

I admire the spiritual accomplishments you've attained in this life, but I just don't know if I'm smart enough to learn and incorporate everything you teach and do. Do others you've met feel incompetent and insecure the way I do?

I believe that many people feel this way, until they've read my books, heard me speak, or felt my arms around them. I'm not yet able to walk on water or through walls, to turn rocks into bread or pebbles into dinner rolls, so please don't put me on a pedestal, okay? My level of confidence comes from being a healer for nearly sixteen years now and meeting countless unimaginable earthly and heavenly situations. I can assure you, however, that you are smart enough to be able to accomplish this and greater things.

To make this easier for you to believe, I'll use two little children as the examples.

Years ago, I took nine months away from my promotional, teaching travels to be the primary caregiver for my grandson.

When Colton was three months old, I opened my heart

and home to him at 6:30 each morning and kept him until 7:00 every night. Even when he was only a month old, I looked into his eyes as I fed him his bottle and he telepathically projected what he was seeing as he looked at me. His mind and mine melded and I viewed the soft pinks and greens of my aura . . . as seen through the eyes of a newborn child. He wasn't viewing my facial features; he was looking at my pretty lights.

He followed behind me daily in his walker, and when he could walk, he was assigned daily chores. It was his job to clean the lint trap on the dryer, and with his child-sized broom, we shared daily cleanup.

We meditated together daily. I taught him to enunciate as he learned to speak, and I have never treated him like a baby *who couldn't understand.* He didn't have the communication skills in the beginning, of course, and was living in an infant body, but his consciousness is God and he was a sponge for information.

As I cooked, I lifted him to see what and how I was preparing meals. I read to him, played, and was affectionate and warm as a granny should be.

At eleven months, Colton toddled up to me at the kitchen table. He swiveled my chair so we were face to face. Lifting my left hand and placing it on his right ear, he leaned his head and my hand to rest upon my lap.

Being empathic, I could literally feel the heat and pain in Colton's ear. Sharply I said, "Colton Lee Henderson, you know **how** to do this yourself and I suggest you do it."

Colton lifted his head from my lap and toddled over to the rug that lay before the sliding-glass door in my kitchen. He laid down upon the rug, placed both his tiny hands upon his ears, closed his eyes, and opened himself to the Presence of God.

Only a few minutes passed and he returned to stand before me. He placed my hand upon his ear again and I felt no further heat or pain.

I never taught Colton *how* to do healings; I merely reminded him that he knew how.

Sixteen years ago, when I became conscious of my healing gift, I was whining to a girlfriend. "Sure I can do healings, write books, and channel directly from a person's soul. But *what if it's just my ego making me think this is what I'm supposed to be doing* and it's not really what God wants me to do?"

My friend Paula laughed and said sarcastically, "Right, Gloria. **You** have the gifts, *but someone else is supposed to do it.*"

With authority, I said, "Well, I don't care. Until I'm given a direct sign from God, I'm not going to do any of it any longer."

Only moments later, Paula's three-year-old grandson, Travis, came into the kitchen and said, "Gloria, I have a headache, will you hold me?"

Paula replied, "Well, baby, Grandma will hold you. . . ."

Travis pointed his little index finger sharply at Paula and said, "I don't want *you* to hold me." He turned and pointed at me and said, "I want *her* to hold me."

I thought his response was darling, as did Paula, but I still wasn't making the connection of the instantaneous response, from Spirit, to my request "for a sign."

I held Travis, rocking and humming. I wasn't trying to *fix* his headache, because as a human, I don't have the power to do so. I was willing to love him, though.

Minutes passed. Travis sat up from my arms, pushed my hands away, and while he was climbing down from my lap, he said, "Thanks. I don't have a headache any more."

Paula and I just looked at each other and laughed. Okay. Okay. Okay. So, "maybe" I am a healer? I put a few more restrictions before Spirit that day, though. "I won't advertise it, don't want to become famous for it, and would prefer no one really finds out about it." Just a few human conditions were placed upon my gifts that day. . . .

You're such a smart hummer; you probably already have this figured out. The gifts weren't given for my personal enjoyment, use, convenience, or income-producing possibilities. The gift was God's and He's the One who would glorify Himself, using me as the instrument.

Had it been up to me, no one would have found out, except for my closest friends and family members.

When you "remember" how to heal yourself or others, are capable of dissolving cancer and helping masses of people, you won't have to advertise. Word of mouth spreads like wildfire and your life is forever changed.

A publisher recently told me, "If you can really do what you say you can in your book *Go Within or Go Without,* we're definitely going to want to publish you." I replied, "Guess what? I really *can* do what I say in that book, but better than that—*so can you,* with awareness." As negotiations continued, I was informed that until I was willing to become famous for being a healer and allow people to come knocking on my door, my writings couldn't be considered by their company. Until then, I had never once thought of becoming famous for my healing talent. Never. Not one time.

Being a healer isn't my destiny. Teaching others how to heal their lives and how to have the direct experience of God is my destiny.

I love it, Glo-bug, that I have this one-to-one attention with you. I feel so fortunate that I'm getting to be your friend and experience all this directly. I wish you could put

your arms around the entire world as you have for me today.

Miracles happen through me. All the time. And call me psychic, but I know that, as you're hearing these stories, you're thinking, "I'd love to have Gloria help me and do a private healing for me and Aunt Bertha, and Uncle Albert, and cousin Shirley, and the postman, and my friend's niece." Most people think I would be an answer to their prayers.

I can be. That's why I invited you to join me on this journey. It's also why I allow God to flood endless, infinite love into my writings so everyone can receive the miracles they seek. But, I'm not here to heal the world; I'm here to teach you how to heal your own world.

Though you may not be conscious of it (yet), *you* have been an answer to someone's prayers. Countless times, I'm sure. And others have been answers to *your* prayers just as many times. I know this from experience. I've watched each of you do loving and kind things for friends, family, strangers, and me. We each can have "bad" days, but the core of us is goodness. We don't have the power to change that spiritual reality. (Thank goodness.)

I believe in you. Whether or not people believe in God doesn't matter, because He believes in us. I also believe in the power of prayer. As a spiritual healer I've daily witnessed the effects of prayer. But I can also verify a lifetime of unanswered prayers, which were actually some of God's greatest gifts. I can speak with authority on both issues.

Gloria, didn't you ever have doubts? Was it always so easy to accept the spiritual experiences, and the miracles? I am one of those people who have to see it to believe it. Did you always have such a trusting nature?

When I began having profound experiences, I was dense as a post. I doubted everything at first and had to see it to believe it, too. But, wow, I certainly discovered the capacity of the Power and Presence quickly. When He asked me to write a book to "Awaken millions and millions of My children from their past slumber of negative beliefs and fears, healing the minds of mankind," I know now that I never had an awareness of how BIG He was referring to.

Regardless of how ignorant my human personality may have been, miracles and mystical experiences, as well as Divine Guidance in the form of dreams and visions, began occurring. Amidst the supernatural occurrences, Jesus appeared one evening and guided me to start writing the experiences down. Teasing, I questioned, "What? Do you think senility will set in early on me?" I assured Him, "I'll never forget. . . ." In a tone, without judgment (and rolling His eyes teasingly), He said, "Just start writing them down, Gloria." I did and the books began.

The first book took approximately three months to write, in between caring for my two toddlers and answering the calls for help from family, friends, and strangers. I didn't have a legal title to counsel and never advertised or handed out business cards; yet, countless people called daily to be uplifted and healed.

After I completed the first book, I sent it to a New York publisher. It was accepted and I recalled it and tore up the contract. **Fear of success.** Two years later, it went to a Denver Publisher and was accepted a second time. Once again, I recalled it and tore up the contract. **Fear of failure.**

So, you DID have fears and doubts, too? I'm feeling better already that what I'm feeling is natural and part of the process.

Not only was I afraid of failure, but I'd met a friend I hadn't seen in a very long time. He asked what I'd been doing since we last saw each other. Proudly I stated, "I've written a book."

"What about?" he asked. I opened my mouth to speak and found only a slurred, frightened version of the word escaping my lips.

"Gaw-w-w-w-w . . ." Dave, of course, was confused and asked, "What's it about?" A second time, I opened my mouth and felt silly and fearful as I repeated, "Gaw-w-w-w-w . . ."

Dave shook his head in confusion and asked, "What's it about, Gloria?" I asked if I could write it down to answer his question and he replied, "Sure."

With pen in hand, I slowly and painfully printed the letters, **G O D.** Dave threw himself back into his chair and began roaring with laughter, which embarrassed me. "You're writing about God?" Quietly and meekly, I replied, "Yes."

Our conversation was a failure because I was too embarrassed to speak further about my book. Every now and then, Dave would burst into another fit of laughter.

Thank God for unanswered prayers. I wasn't ready to be published. I couldn't even say the word "God." How would I have been able to promote the book or answer questions in an audience or interview setting? If a loved one could spark such embarrassment and insecurity, what would a skeptic or cruel person be able to achieve?

The books continued, one a year, and were filled with modern-day miracles and spiritual teachings. As I look back at the writings, I am so thankful the first eight books never went to press. Not that the information isn't worthwhile and valid, but I must be objective about my writing style. My journey continues as the universe demands that I

continue to grow and hopefully my writing style is pro-
gressing, as well.

I shared the importance of what is termed "Unanswered
Prayers," only to give you an awareness that as you sit and
pray and think you're not being heard—more than likely
you are, and it wouldn't be to your highest good to receive
what you are asking for. As an eternal optimist, in those situations when I don't get what I think I wanted, I'm reminded, **God must love me so very, very much, because
something even better is forthcoming.** From my personal
experience, God never withholds love in any form. Only
humans do that. Long ago, probably about the moment of
creation, He gave all He had to give. As a human, we just
need to raise our awareness to recognize that.

My goal is to teach the world how to heal their lives. In
sixteen years, I've taken every opportunity to teach one individual at a time . . . a person sitting next to me on an air-
plane, a child in the street, an audience in an auditorium,
convicts behind bars, and you . . . here, today. I'm a mere
pebble in a pond, creating a ripple effect today, and with
your help as you incorporate these teachings, it can become
the wave of the future. You see, one person can make a difference and that person is . . . **you.**

4

A Lightbearer for All Nations, a Messenger for All People

Dr. Glo-bug, you say I can make a difference in the world, and I suppose in my individual way, I do. Did you ever think, while growing up, that you would have such an impact on society?

As a child, I "knew" I was supposed to do something important for the world, but I didn't know how that could ever happen unless the world could meet me in the closet or beneath my bed. All I consciously understood was that I wanted to grow up and be a wife and mother. And by the way, I feel that these roles are indeed great accomplishments.

I, as many other students of your teachings, do admire how you have God in one hand and meatloaf in the other. You have the ability to make the mystical side of life sound ordinary and accessible. Also, you're just like us . . . paying bills, raising kids, and dealing with real-life experiences of pain, sadness, illness, and fear—and yet, you seem to find a spiritual meaning behind all of it.

My spiritual awakening came at age thirty-two. I awoke one morning and was aware I was a healer, and was asked to write a book to awaken millions of His children. My telephone never stopped ringing, though I didn't advertise. Perhaps it was because I didn't charge. In any case, my mundane life as a housewife and a mother had definitely changed. And I didn't necessarily want it to. Denial was a comfortable place to be.

During an afternoon quiet time while my four kids were in school, I had a mystical experience. My mind opened to a wide-screen TV and two Lightbeings appeared in my inner vision. While the revelation was occurring, I saw myself slowly approach the heavenly beings, in awe of the feeling and beauty present. Only in my fantasies had I ever dreamed or envisioned such splendor. Standing before me was an opportunity most people can only dream of, a chance to know my true purpose for living.

It was as though my feet floated above a royal carpet. "Perhaps this was symbolic," I thought. Throughout my physical life (or previous lives?), I had already taken all the steps necessary to arrive at this moment of eternity. I knelt in reverence before the adorned and radiant couple, awaiting my anointing (and I wasn't even sure what that word meant as it filled my mind).

I raised my eyes to look at the woman before me. She was cloaked in a robe of pure white light. Until now, I had never seen such an exquisite, clear complexion and inner beauty. It radiated outward. The Divine Messenger handed me a lighted white candle and as I received and accepted it, the message followed, *You are a Lightbearer for all nations.*

I was filled with intense joy to carry the light for my fellow human beings and found my attention drawn to the male Messenger to my right. He placed a second, lighted white candle into my opened palm, which mystically transformed into a simple scroll. My destiny became clear as he completed the spiritual guidance, *And a messenger for all people.*

I quickly and excitedly unrolled the scroll, to look upon the message I was to give to humankind. The parchment melted away into nothingness. . . . I was confused. I asked, "But, what is the message I'm being asked to share?" As the couple disappeared from my inner vision, the words lingered behind—*The message is within your soul.*

What a beautiful experience. Do you think I'll ever experience anything like this, and if I do, will it terrify me?

I'm sure you will begin experiencing this, and many other paranormal events as you close your eyes and open your individual mind to the Presence of God. And, no, you won't need to fear when it happens. You will be filled with a brilliant, intense warmth of what I call "liquid fire" that flows throughout your veins. You will know, then, that you are experiencing God directly and that there's nothing in God that can hurt you.

At the time of this experience, however, I was more confused than ever. Where was my soul? How was I to retrieve the message "within my soul" if I didn't know how to even locate its existence? Who would you ask, if seeking directions, how to locate your soul? I wish my books had been available to me as I was seeking, growing, doubting, fearing, and having to learn to trust and develop faith in those things not seen with physical eyes.

I had been busy minding my own daily business, totally non-religious and not even knowing the word "spiritual." I was frustrated that my journey was beginning to take me on a daily walk through the twentieth- and twenty-first-century worlds and I didn't have a teacher "with skin on" to help me take those steps. I was being prepared to live and teach as a modern-day apostle, offering understanding to an age-old mysterious message, and all I could do was trust, moment-to-moment, in an Invisible World.

How did you learn to balance the physical and spiritual so easily?

A balancing act wasn't easy, having one foot in the physical world and having such profound spiritual experiences, pretending I was living an ordinary existence. One afternoon, a message continued to fill my thoughts: *Time is running out.* It frightened me, but I was too afraid to ask what it meant. Throughout the day, the one-liner continued to repeat itself in my mind. Finally, I screamed at the top of my silent lungs, *What? Does this mean I'm going to physically die?* An inner, bold message followed, *No. Time is running out on attempting to live an ordinary life with extraordinary power.*

Wow. Now I really was scared. I felt very alone, unaware that the world was being prepared by many messengers and healers.

As I awoke one morning, the first thought I had before my dream melted away was, "I am One with God and within that Oneness, infinite power stands behind me." I remember back to that moment as I looked to the ceiling over my bed and said, "Yo, God. Don't you think that's a little heavy for first thing in the morning? Wouldn't a simple, 'Good morning, Gloria,' do?"

Dr. Glo-bug, I think it's so wonderful how you can even tease when you're talking to God. Most people in this world are taught to fear that Presence, and you make Him sound like your best friend. Just knowing that we don't need to be frightened of "God's wrath" can bring peace to humanity, and me. Please continue with your story.

Although the one-liner was pretty and I was able to use it in several of my writings, two years would go by before I felt the full impact of its meaning.

I had begun the "Body for Life Workout" as presented by best-selling author Bill Phillips. I was completing my final day of the twelve-week program. Finishing the lower body workout and lying upon the floor, getting ready to do my forty-eight crunches and forty-eight weighted leg lifts, the muscles in my legs began to quiver. I was used to the feeling, of course, but then the quiver turned into a river. Within my legs, it felt like a torrent of flooding waters rushing into me. My legs shook with the intense energy, but when I looked at the outer appearance of my physical legs, they weren't even moving.

This experience occurred for approximately eight minutes and when I could stand, I went to phone my husband, Kirk, at work. I began the conversation, "Remember two years ago when I was awakened with the thought, *I am one with God and within that Oneness, infinite power stands behind me?*" Kirk recalled that experience because I had spoken of it often. In this conversation, I continued, "That was a beautiful one-liner, BUT TODAY I FELT IT. I need to stop thinking I'm a four-foot-eleven petite person, because I am an immense spirit." I knew something very big was about to happen in the outer realm. My spirit had been renewed for something that would benefit the whole of humanity.

Could you share some of your beginning experiences with me? I feel so hungry to grow and learn. Also, Kirk is right, Gloria, you do overwhelm people. You do talk faster than a speeding bullet and I know you have so many things to share with the world. You never know how long you're going to have with someone at any given point, so you want to tell them everything you can NOW.

But, I want to share my opinion concerning that. It's like a person's first spiritual banquet. We have never met anyone who "can do all this," and we want to hear everything we can. We may not be able to absorb it all at once, but in book form or future guest speaking, we'll go back to those sources and eat leftovers until we do get it, as we can understand more.

Talk about *me* teasing *you* about being a motormouth. Look what I just did, too. Please continue. Tell me about some of your initial experiences.

In the beginning years, I practiced and found I could swivel and rock a chair in my living room (with my mind). I knew how to astral project and knew it occurred the moment before I'd drift off to sleep. I could project my energy, at will, without quieting my mind. I could "see" across the miles because in reality, there is no distance. We are where our thoughts are.

Once I was opened to the Presence of God within me, I could do all these things without reading a book or being taught how to do it. I could just do it. Of course, it took "a minute" to grow into the awareness of all that was occurring.

I also became aware of my gifts of empathy, telepathy, and intuition. I had no idea anyone could do these things, let alone me.

While preparing dinner one evening, I thoughtlessly used my fingers to flatten a tortilla in the hot, bubbling oil. As soon as I realized what I had done, I thought, "That wasn't very bright." I sat on the kitchen floor and, intuitively guided, I felt no fear. I touched each burned finger, one at a time while speaking an attribute of God aloud. Hope. Peace. Divine Love. Compassion. Joy. Courage, and so on. Ten touches, two to each finger, healed the burns. No ice, no pain, no fear.

Put yourself in my shoes for a moment. You just want to be a housewife and mom. You don't mind writing a book about miracles because they could inspire the world. Imagine being unaware of any other healers . . . and none of your friends are having mystical experiences. No common ground.

I imagine all this was a very lonely time for you, Gloria. I wish I could have been there for you.

Thank you so much. I wish you had been there for me, too. For the first ten years, I was able to be as silent as possible and then it was time to go public. LuAnn Stallcop owned a newspaper in Spokane, Washington. She heard about me and drove to Montana to interview me. As we sat having lunch, it was exactly noon and I fell back into my seat and grabbed my heart. "LuAnn, someone you know just had their heart healed through me." We finished the interview and she returned to Spokane, calling the only woman she knew who had a heart problem.

As their conversation began, her friend Carolyn excitedly remarked, "Today, at exactly eleven o'clock, I was standing in the kitchen. A beautiful and intense light filled my heart and I fell back against the refrigerator and **I knew my heart was healed.**" LuAnn laughed and said, "Yeah . . . well, I was with the woman in Montana when it happened—and it was exactly noon her time when it occurred.

While I was healing an eight-year-old boy from brain, lung, and spinal cancer, I laid him on the floor to make him as comfortable as possible during the healing session. Being empathic, I could feel so much tremendous heat within him, as well as the pain. Tears were flowing from my eyes and soaking the pillow beneath my head. I said, "Dustin, if you want to cry, I'll cry with you—I can feel the pain and it hurts so badly."

Tearfully he asked, "But, why would you want to feel my pain?" I responded, "Dustin, if I can help you and others carry the pain, until I can get it dissolved . . . it's less pain that you have to feel." In sobs, which broke his parents' hearts, as well as mine, he cried out, "But, why would you or anyone want to feel the amount of pain that I do?"

I can only imagine this type of healing gift, Gloria. We all need this awareness, because each of us can meet someone in pain on the street, next door, through the media, or in our own home. We need you to share this information with the world so we can dissolve this needless suffering and strife. I'll bet you do scare the hell out of people and overwhelm them when you attempt to make them aware that it's possible. It's a priceless gift, but along with that gift, I'm sure it brings many frustrating side effects—the challenges, adversity, and misunderstandings because of wording or beliefs.

Before a group of people, I'll honestly admit, "I need you all a whole helluva lot more than you think you need me. I need to make you aware that you, too, can perform these and greater works. I need you to teach those in your circles of family and friends. I need you to help make a difference in this world.

I'm willing, Glo-bug, and others are, too.

Let me share one more story, and then I will pull off at the next rest area for a smoke and bathroom break. One evening my son, crying with growing pains, awakened me. I snuggled him to my breasts and whispered, "D.W., just take a deep breath and relax." He cried pitifully, "I can't,

Mamma, it hurts too bad." An inner Voice asked me to place my right index and middle fingers upon D.W.'s forehead and to state aloud, "Peace be with you." Having been awakened from a sound sleep, I didn't have any interfering, logical thoughts that it wouldn't work. I did as guided and immediately, D.W. stopped crying and fell asleep at my side.

I silently said, "Thanks, God" and fell back to sleep. However, as I awoke the next morning, a replay of the experience was the first thought in my mind. *Wow. Think of all the possibilities.* I recalled the miracle throughout the day. It was just too awesome to ignore. That afternoon, I was on my way across Sacramento during rush hour, to be interviewed as a possible guest speaker for an AIDS group. Along the way, I had an urge to stop at a metaphysical bookstore. I didn't need anything, however, and if I stopped, I'd be late for my appointment. Spirit hammered me with the repeated thoughts and I submitted, although I had no reason to stop.

As I stepped into the bookstore, I hugged the owner and asked if her daughter, Gina, was available. I had only met the mother and daughter once and didn't consciously know why I was asking for Gina. Guided to the back office, as I rounded the corner, I could hear Gina crying.

"Are you okay?" I asked. "No," she sobbed, "I just burned my finger and there's no ice in the building and it's throbbing." Through blurry tears, she cried louder, "It's killing me."

Quickly telling Gina what had occurred with my son the prior evening, I said, "Here, maybe I should try doing it to you." Pretending I was one of the Three Stooges, as if I was going to poke her in the eyes with my two fingers, at the last moment . . . I gently touched her forehead and stated aloud, "Peace be with you." Her shriek startled me as she screeched, "My finger doesn't hurt any more." I remarked, "You're kidding? Cool. Gotta go." And, I made it to my appointment on time.

Years of tasting and smelling purity (which is a combination of the scent of Ivory soap, roses, and the smell after a thunderstorm), and watching as miracles occurred, were the writings of my books. In the first two months, I had counted more than one thousand miracles and none of them had anything to do with food, clothing, shelter, supportive friends, or family. They were outright miracles. My daily mantra had teasingly become, "When all else fails . . . plan for a miracle."

5

You Deserve a Break Today

Let's get out and stretch our legs. Would you feel comfortable sitting on that shady grass, under the trees, to have the snack? Ahhh, breathe in that beautiful forest cedar and pine scent. What a beautiful world we live in.

I have some power bars, fresh fruit, a choice of strawberry licorice, or some cheddar-flavored rice cakes. I also have a selection of sodas and water. Feel free to help yourself to as much as you'd like.

I'd like to take some time to help explain the process of opening yourself to the Presence of God. As you're sitting there, close your eyes, slowly tilt your head back, as if looking up to the sky. Slowly rotate your head over your right shoulder, down and across your upper chest, and continue the slow rotation of your head over the left shoulder and back to the original position.

Did you hear what resembles the sound of gravel as you rotated your head? At the base of the back of the head is the pineal gland, the master gland of the body. It's through this gland that electricity/energy/love (whichever you feel most comfortable calling it), comes through to feed and maintain your body.

When we get stressed, tense, or scared, we tighten the muscles in this area and it creates "energy blocks" that disallow the electricity to fully sustain us. I don't want you to overdo this exercise, perhaps just a few times throughout the day. When you hear the "gravel" breaking, you will experience a heightened sense of energy and spontaneous healing (if you so need it).

I describe these energy blockages as something similar to a garden hose. If you kink the hose in half, water stops flowing. Well, if you have an energy blockage in your body, it creates pain because it's not getting the light/electricity it needs for balance, healing, and harmony. Each time you hear the gravel, again, the kink in the garden hose/physical body is dissolving and the energy flows and manifests what we call "a miracle." Healing can be so simple.

Did you ever see the original *Karate Kid* movie? Remember when Daniel was painting the fence, unknowingly building the motion and muscle for his karate moves? His mentor, Mr. Miaggi, had been out fishing while Daniel was working. Unaware he was getting trained, he became angry that his teacher was out playing while he was working. And besides, his shoulder now hurt from the repetitive motion.

Mr. Miaggi rubbed his hands together and placed the right hand on Daniel's shoulder and a spontaneous healing occurred. Later, at the end of the movie, Mr. Miaggi rubbed his hands together again and laid them upon Daniel's leg, to heal it, so he could fight the last fight to win.

When you rub your hands together, it turns on the energy. Laying hands upon a pain is successful in its own right; however, if you add a twist (no pun intended), by slowly rotating your head, the energy blockage in that area will be quickly dissolved and immediate healing can occur.

During this break, I'd like you to also work on the pain you have in your right knee. I've empathied it the entire time we were talking, but I didn't want to dissolve it for you. I wanted to show you how very simple this technique is. Rub your hands together and place the right hand about an inch above your pain. Move your hand lower on your leg and feel the difference in the hot or cold sensation. Slowly move your hand to your upper thigh, sensing the energy of that area, as well.

Now, return to the knee again, just to feel the temperature difference. It is amazingly different, isn't it, from the energy of your nonpained upper and lower leg?

Now, once again, rub your hands together and place them upon your knee. Lean your head back and slowly rotate your head, across the right shoulder, down over the upper chest, over the left shoulder and back to the original position.

Take a deep breath and exhale.

In your inner vision, it's dark. However, with your eyes closed, the darkness will begin to lighten to a shade of grey. It may turn colors of dirty yellow or green. Take another slow, deep breath and exhale.

Within your inner vision, the colors may now change, slowly or quickly, from the yellow or green, to pink, blue, red (if the knee severely hurts), and then you may begin seeing a violet ray in your mind's eye. Take another deep breath and exhale as you give thanks, because your knee, more than likely, no longer hurts. When it no longer hurts you, it doesn't hurt me either. When I'm healing someone across the miles, I become One with them, and when I no longer feel their pain, it's dissolved within them, as well. It's because there is really only One body. God's body, manifesting as bazillions of manifestations of the One.

Why do people make healing harder than it needs to be?

The violet Light is the color we see when transformation from human to Divine is occurring. God created all that is and He looked upon it and called it "good." (He didn't call it "good and bad.") Everything, including our perfect health, wealth, and well-being is already established within His mind. Our false beliefs of two powers, of good and evil, have clouded our perception of spiritual reality. When we open our mind to the violet light, we are no longer the blind leading the blind. Our vision is restored. We now can experience faith, in its truest form because WE CAN SEE the Presence of God, expressing through this ray. We will witness perfection made manifest in our physical worlds as we open ourselves to that Presence of All Good.

Gloria, I am simply amazed. First, that you felt my pain and knew I had a problem with my knee without me telling you, and second, that I was able to heal it myself. My knee no longer hurts.

I know. Miracles, in my beginning years, did dazzle me too. I spent half my career walking around saying, "You're kidding?" every time another one occurred through me. The reason I could feel the pain is because I am One with God, which constitutes my Oneness with all spiritual beings, ideas, and creations.

For just a moment, try this exercise. If you can see what I'm saying, that's great. If not, that's okay, too.

Imagine a golden light around you. Now, see a golden light around all of this forest. Expand the golden light to encompass this state, in fact, how about the entire United States? Continue to visualize a golden light around the entire earth. Stretch yourself to imagine a golden light around the entire universe, and all the infinite universes that you could fathom.

Everything you just saw with golden light around it is already established in perfect form within the mind of God. Not something you have to create, something that already Is. Everything you will ever need, have ever needed, or think you need now is already established and thought into expression within the Divine Mind. And, since you are also within that Mind, this means that your Oneness is already established as "having it" without taking human mental processes to make it come forth. Awareness of Oneness is your key to smooth sailing.

This has been a nice break, but it's probably time to get going. I've reserved a table for two at the lake in Coeur d'Alene, Idaho, for our lunch. Do you have any questions about what I just taught?

Yes, Gloria, I do have a couple of questions. What if I don't see the purple or violet Light? Does this mean that I haven't raised my consciousness and that I can't personally expect a miracle?

Wow. What a great question. I'm so glad you asked if you were concerned for even a second. No, you don't have to actually see the light before this life-saving tip can manifest itself as a miracle. You will undoubtedly feel the warmth from your hands and perhaps even a tingling as you feel the energy flow through you. When you can actually see the light, however, you are no longer second-guessing if you have made the Direct connection to the Divine State of Consciousness.

Once you have opened your mind for the violet Light/Presence of God to flow through your individual awareness, the "Christ" within you is "on the scene," and perfection will be made visible. Thank you so much for allowing me to clearly express what you can expect. The light isn't available to use; "It" uses your mind as an avenue of awareness. The light isn't called forth into expression just to heal your boo-boos either. Every time you open yourself to that Divinity within you, it expresses outwardly as everything you need, usually before you're conscious that you need it. You have better health, happier relationships, and abundance in all forms—joy, and inner peace. Every part of your life is God's vehicle to live through you, to touch you with His majesty, glory, and His Divine Idea of what is a "good life."

You deserved a break today . . . but you deserve one every day. His way is the High-way, and speaking of that, let's get back on the road.

6

As Above, So Below

Gloria, when you just said the words "High-way," it, of course, made me think of heaven. We're all taught that when we die, we'll go to heaven or hell; yet, religions have inspired us to experience heaven upon earth. I'm also confused about prayer, could you please explain about that, too?

Before I became spiritual, I had literal nightmares that someone would ask me to say grace before a meal. I didn't know how to pray to God. I didn't have any fancy words and had no inclination to memorize someone else's. Every night I would say my bedtime prayer, asking God to bless all those I loved and saying the routine "Amen." The two times I saw fit to pray, I merely used my own words and spoke from my heart.

Actually, I always believed that prayer was "listening," not talking. The prayers we state silently or verbally can bring our attention and focus to God, but once we've raised our consciousness to that level, if we remain silent, He sends a direct impulse to us in the form of words or intuition . . . answering our silent prayers.

Many years ago, every single thing had gone perfectly from sunup to sundown. I felt such gratitude, and my heart was heaped with love. As I lay in bed that evening, rather than my blah, blah, blah, bless 'em prayer, I decided to write a letter to God in white typed lettering. It began, "Dear God," and then listed all those things that I had experienced with such appreciation for the day. At the end of the long-winded "thank-you letter," I signed off, "Love, Gloria."

Immediately, a reply in white typed lettering followed. "Dear Gloria, You're welcome! Love, God." I went to sleep with a smile on my face that evening.

See what I mean, Gloria? You can make even a simple prayer and personal experiences sound so natural and sweet. So many of us don't know how to pray. At least, I don't know if I'm "doing it right" or if God even hears my prayers. I repeat memorized prayers, such as "The Lord's Prayer" and the bedtime prayer, but other prayers seem so rehearsed and mechanical, which sounds like I'm in judgment concerning them.

I found that the best way is just to speak from my heart, just as if I'm talking directly to a friend, like you, whether that comes in the form of a book or in speaking personally.

In watching the recent Olympics, I was explaining to my husband that I was never good at competitive sports. Whenever I found myself in a race against others, and noticed my dad watching in the crowd, I'd stop dead in my tracks and walk off the field.

For piano recitals, I would have the tune memorized perfectly and begin playing, but again, if I noticed my dad paying attention, I would flub up. He never once placed strong expectations on me to succeed, and was proud of me regardless of anything I attempted to do, whether I saw them as failures or successes. I wanted to please him and have his approval, but of course, I already had it.

It's the same with God. Sometimes I feel like I let Him down, but He just goes on loving me regardless. He doesn't place great expectations on me, He accepts me for who I am.

I believe the reason I don't think I'll let my (earthly) father down, in writing books and letters to the world, doing healings, being a public speaker or healer, is because in doing those things, I'm not in competition with anyone. I'm free to just be myself. I'm not trying to be better than someone else, I'm happy being who I am. I wasn't always happy with me, of course, and sometimes we're harder on ourselves than we ever would be with another.

I don't know if I have time for self-realization, Gloria. I have such a busy life and so many demands placed upon me. I just had the thought, though, you probably are praying and talking and listening to God, even as you're mopping the floor, aren't you?

Yes, I am. The daily workout program of author Bill Phillips that I follow—and continue to make it a way of life—I call my "I Love Me Program." I am willing to take an hour a day to become physically strong and healthy, allowing me to love myself as much as I am willing to love others. Loving oneself always seemed selfish or vain, but I found that until I loved me—others couldn't. Until I appreciated myself—others wouldn't. We find we have so many fears associated with ourselves, others, and life around us.

I don't know that I was ever afraid of the version of God that religions teach. I was too ignorant to understand that I should be. But, since He's invisible, it was hard to track Him down and look Him in the eyes, until I realized that every person I meet—when I see the Light in their eyes, I am looking face to face at Him.

In September of 1987, I closed my eyes; my inner vision opened and Jesus appeared. He replied, "Because you have such a strong desire to know how it was that I walked on water—tonight, it is with great pleasure that I give you this awareness." He took my hand and together, we teleported to the ocean. I was completely aware that my body had been transported and it wasn't my imagination.

Danielle awoke crying and I returned immediately to my home. She had an earache and as I held her, the pain she had felt dissolved immediately. I returned sadly, however, to my bedroom. As I walked down the hall to go back to bed, I thought, "Of all times for her to get sick." I believed I had missed a great opportunity of learning.

I no sooner had closed my eyes when Jesus reappeared, commenting, "I fulfill all promises." With that bold statement, He gently took my hand and we were once again standing at the edge of the ocean. In remembering this experience, I must share the teachings from that evening.

HEAVEN ON EARTH

One evening, Jesus appeared and stood before me. His voice shattered the silence with great wisdom and authority as He spoke, "Because you have such a strong desire to know how it was that I walked on water, tonight it is with great pleasure that I give you this awareness."

He gently took my hand and we transcended time and space. Together, we stood on the sands, overlooking the ocean.

Beyond time, He and I had entered the realm of the

Spiritual Kingdom. Golden light filtered through a blue haze. Off in the sunset, it was difficult to distinguish the sky's horizon from the water's edge where the sea and sky met. I questioned silently if this was where heaven and earth could meet?

We faced each other as His left hand reached up to touch my shoulder. His right hand raised as He gestured toward the waves, replying, "I never looked to man, nor earth, to support Me." The salted sea baptized our feet with warm foam and He continued, "I looked only to Infinite Spirit's Love. . . ."

In that solemn moment, the revelation awoke me with a Soul Call of total truth and knowingness. I was filled with a glorious warmth and strength I had never known in the physical life. I knew, in my heart, I would never again look to the world of form, a paycheck, a mate, or food as my eternal sustaining strength.

I now knew of One Power and Intelligence forever governing my life. My Oneness with God constituted my Oneness with all spiritual beings, ideas, and creations. The ocean, as well as my life, were One with God, and there was nothing in God that could hurt me.

I didn't need to step upon the water to prove my faith or understanding to a world or to a God I'd been taught about. I no longer sought or needed the approval of others, for in that moment of complete acceptance, I believed in my Oneness.

Jesus turned to hug me and we melded as two souls became One. Hereafter, I would give as I had been given. I, too, looked only to Infinite Spirit's Love . . .

What a beautiful experience, Dr. Glo-bug. As you were retelling of your experience, I felt as if I was right there

with you. My heart feels so full of love, but I have to admit, my mind is racing . . . wanting even more. It's almost as if I've been spiritually starved and I'm so very hungry.

As you continue to practice the Presence, you'll find yourself completely fulfilled and filled full. Also, you are aware, aren't you that I'm not attempting to change your mind, beliefs, attitudes, or opinions? I'm just sharing my experiences, and like the Twelve-Step Program, take what you like from these teachings and leave the rest. If I must apologize, I will, if I'm getting too close or personal with you. I feel as if we are best friends, and I feel safe enough to say whatever it is that I'm thinking and feeling. That's how I pray, too. I open my heart and allow whatever feelings are there to come forth.

I think most people are scared to be honest with God with the way they feel, unaware that He knows how you really feel. We're not fooling anyone, except maybe ourselves. Maybe I'm extremely ignorant, but I never felt bad about going to God to have a "bitch session." If I went to a friend in the physical, I would always take the chance that it would get passed on to others through gossip or betrayal. I never feared that God would hurt me. I never believed He had it in Him to hurt anyone. I always thought, "everyone believed in God," and was amazed to meet so many who didn't. Or, at least they said they didn't.

It's time for ole Dr. Glo-bug to lighten things up. During my supernatural experiences, I met many people who questioned how I knew that it was really Jesus who was appearing to me. "After all," they counseled, "it could be the devil disguised as Jesus." First of all, I never believed in Satan—I never believed that God, being God, would create opposition to Himself. I attempted repeatedly to console these people that when God appears, whether He wears the face

of Jesus, Buddha, Krishna, or any other spiritual personage
... *you know by the amount of unconditional love present.*

After being asked so many times, however, I decided to
ask Jesus on one of His visits. "How do I know you're really
Jesus?" He replied, "How do I know you're really Gloria?"

**I do believe God speaks through our awareness at a level
we can understand. He does give some elusive messages,
however, that sometimes drive me nuts, attempting to figure them out, or "getting it" as they reveal themselves in
the physical world.**

**I do want a personal relationship with Spirit and I do
believe it is possible. In fact, after listening to you—with
awareness—it can be the most natural thing in the world.**

If I could name but two frustrations I have with the
teachings in this world, they would have to be these:

> 1. We are taught the Golden Rule, "Do unto others as
> you would have them do unto you," but we don't under-
> stand that the Golden Rule is actually karmic law of
> "what goes around comes around." Those actions we
> take toward another are setting the karmic law into mo-
> tion; therefore, those things we do—we are actually
> doing to ourselves. We tend to forget that we have per-
> formed negative acts toward another and appear sur-
> prised when we find ourselves in uncomfortable
> situations. We cry out, "What did I ever do that was so
> bad to deserve this? The answer, of course, is we did it
> first and it's "payback time."
>
> It's frustrating to me that, as children, we're not taught
> the total truth of the Golden Rule early enough in life to
> incorporate it completely into our lives. Simple under-
> standing of the reasons why we shouldn't try to cheat
> our neighbor, gossip, lie, or the various other situations

we find ourselves in shouldn't need to come forth in the Commandments, without the complete spiritual understanding offered, as well.

2. We have not been taught how to have a close and personal relationship with God. We were taught "about Him," and read "about Him," but we weren't given awareness of how to go about it. Also, we have been taught to fear God. That's like telling us to fear Love, Itself.

That's why what you're doing is so important, Doc. You're giving us awareness, through examples. In the Bible we received parables . . . but without illustrations of how to incorporate them into our lives. We don't know, without direct experience or teachings, how it FEELS to have God in our life.

During a recent workshop, one of the participants had M.S. and arrived in a sitting walker. During the first process of teaching, she was aligned with a woman who would be the healer, and the woman with M.S. would be the healee. While taking the break between the turnaround where the healee would become the healer, this couple called my attention to a situation that had arisen.

The woman with M.S. was crying and frightened. She had gone completely paralyzed, and I remarked, "How wonderful!" She barked, "No, it's not wonderful—this is the next stage of M.S. and what if this healing just accelerated me to that point?"

I explained that what she was feeling was the Presence of God and not to be frightened. I explained several situations where my arms, up to my elbows, go completely numb while Spirit is working through me. It took several minutes to allow the woman's fears to dissolve.

We completed the turnaround and then I asked each

couple to stand before all present to share their experiences. I can easily tell you that I can do this and so can you, but to hear repeated "first time" results allows the audience to understand, "Yes, I can do this, too."

When it came time for this couple to come forth, the women touched fingertips, rather than the full support of holding hands, walking forth together to the front of the room. The woman who "had" M.S. replied tearfully, "Oh, my God, I haven't walked in a very long time."

When people first begin feeling the Presence of God, it does frighten them because they don't understand the intensity of His Love. The pain they feel is merely the resistance they are creating . . . they, themselves, are creating an opposition to Him. When fear is felt, a silent "Oh yeah, this too is God" can dissolve the fear and allow Him to purify our consciousness, which will directly manifest miracles in our lives.

I awoke at 6:00 A.M. today, just like every other day and kissed Kirk good-bye. I took a few quiet moments to say my daily opening prayer, "Good morning, God, I love you. I welcome you in every appearance today." Because God is my consciousness, that means that every single thing that touches my mind, body, and experience today **is God, but appearing in many forms.**

I feel so safe with your teachings, Gloria. I admit, though, if I ever saw fear on your face—I'd know I was in deep *doo-doo*. You've teleported, had out-of-body experiences, and witnessed miracles. Are there other things we might experience as we continue to expand our awareness?

In 1987 I witnessed my first aport, which is an item transported from the unseen dimensions into the physical dimension. Until this experience occurred, I had only read of these occurrences in the Bible. The Master Jesus had healed and fed the multitudes, with baskets of leftover bread and fish. If you remember, He blessed and gave thanks for that which already existed and all those present feasted . . . through His state of consciousness of abundance and the knowingness **that it already existed and all He had to do was call it forth.**

At the time of this experience, I was visiting my sister, Sheila, in Denver. Her boss, Myra, had been listening to Sheila tell of my mystical experiences and had requested to meet me. She was a skeptic, but willing to listen.

Minutes before Myra arrived, I had vacuumed and dusted Sheila's living room, tidying it in preparation of our visitor. Coming from California, I had been unfamiliar with snow, and I felt a warm glow within me as I stared out to the winter wonderland of the white that was quietly falling. I imagined that at least three inches had fallen, and we were told it would continue throughout the night.

I went to check on the sleeping kids. The room they'd been playing in was a total wreck, and in the dimly lit room, I was clearing a path of toys just to bend and kiss each child. (They were going to be VERY BUSY in the morning, cleaning that mess up.)

The doorbell rang and I answered it, greeting Myra and introducing myself. Sheila joined us and hung Myra's coat on a peg near the door. As we seated ourselves, the conversation began immediately with Myra playing "Twenty Questions" with me.

I never actually asked anyone to believe me, without having an actual experience and offered to share a paranormal experience with Myra. The things that were happening in my life were extremely uncommon.

I closed my eyes and saw a home within my vision. I felt as though I was being taken on a guided tour of the house, describing in detail as I was taken up a wooden staircase, turning left at the top of the stairs, opening a door and viewing the curtains, bedspread, and entire inside of the room and closet. Myra, in quiet awe, replied, "That's the home I was raised in."

I was guided, within the vision, to take Myra down to a river where she would meet her deceased father. Hand-in-hand, Myra and I, in the vision, walked across a bridge, turned to the left, and walked with Jesus toward a man sitting quietly alone on the shore, fishing. The man was Myra's father, and he gave her a message that concerned something only the two of them knew. The father and daughter hugged and Jesus escorted us back across the bridge.

As both Myra and I opened our eyes, her skepticism became more pronounced. She believed the experience was just a hoax of the imagination. She couldn't believe any of it had taken place. She suggested that she had told me too much to begin with, but it was impossible for me to know these events.

My only consolation was that we had just met. Myra had told me nothing. I knew, from experience, Myra was reacting from fear. I had seen it so many times before.

Myra nervously replied that she needed to leave. As she stood to walk toward the front door to retrieve her coat, something on the bottom of her shoe snagged the carpet. She lifted her foot and pulled a rusty fishhook from the sole of her shoe.

I knew the hook was an aport, but Myra defended that she must have picked it up on her walk up Sheila's driveway. Remember there were three inches of new-fallen snow, which had just carpeted Denver? Myra was trying to make some human and physical sense of this experience and implied she had snagged the fishhook inside Sheila's home. But remember I had vacuumed before her arrival? Sheila stated that she didn't own any fishing equipment.

It was an aport, a gift from Spirit, for Myra and her disbelief of "these and greater works." Sheila and I hung the fishhook above her kitchen sink as a treasure from the spiritual kingdom.

I'm beginning to see humanity's pattern, Gloria. "As above, so below" are words we mention in church services and prayers, wanting to have heaven and earth become as one. But, we pray and ask for miracles and greater wonders, and when it occurs, it frightens us and we continue to disbelieve.

Dr. Glo-bug, as you explain these experiences, although I may have disbelieved this myself, I am listening to my heart—I CAN HEAR IT—and it's saying that you're not trying to pull anything over on anyone. You're just saying it the way it is. In fact, I feel like I'm in heaven, myself, right this moment.

As a matter of fact, my friend, you are. . . .

7
Family Ties . . .

My husband, Kirk, and others tell me that I overwhelm people, at times. I don't mean to. All these things are just my life. Over the years, however, I am discovering how much I should tell a person at one time. Once I've reached their possible "overload/too much input level," I have an intuitive knowingness that tells me to bring their heads out of the clouds and get their feet back on earth. About now would be a good time.

In fact, I learned (the hard way), NOT to talk about my life while someone is cutting my hair or taking care of my banking needs. Through speaking, I'd raise their awareness and they'd go "outta body . . . back in ten minutes" on me. I'd walk out with VERY short hair or financial errors on my account.

I'll bet your life is such a hoot at times, Gloria. I think it would be fun to be your friend and listen to all your miracle stories as they happen, instead of having to wait until they come out in book form or when you speak publicly.

I'm sure not everyone would agree. Most people don't find me as simply dang adorable as Kirk or you . . . In saying that, I remember an experience that occurred with my ex-brother-in-law, Dennis. For years I'd been sharing my mystical events, and it was all a bit much for Dennis to swallow. He believed I had "some" gift, but didn't believe it was a spiritual healing gift. He thought I had a gift of making anyone feel special and loved. He also boldly shared one day, after listening to some of my spiritual experiences, "I don't know if I'll ever believe these things, unless I actually am witness to something, myself."

One morning, the phone rang and it was Dennis. He began the conversation, "Gloria, I swear to God I'm telling you the truth. I swear to God I was sober. . . ." I interrupted his attempts of excusing what he was about to say.

"Dennis, of all people, you don't have to convince me of anything. What happened?"

He took a breath before he spoke. "Last night, an energy force field came into my bedroom. It was so strong; it actually rolled me up against the wall. A voice, **aloud,** said, "Gloria's going to do it in 1992—**tell her.**"

I laughed and said, "Dennis, stuff like this happens to me all the time. *What is it I'm going to do in 1992?*"

With full honesty in his voice, he said, "I don't know. "They" didn't tell me that."

("Thanks for nothing, Dennis.")

By the way, while I'm thinking about it, I swear . . . or I talk about earth things such as smoking or drinking, or tell an off-color joke, using them as tools to ground a person. I would not be a responsible "healer/instrument" if I allowed people to heighten their consciousness and then attempt to do something physical such as driving or using a knife in their kitchen. We can attain that level of consciousness, but it is pointless if we can't incorporate it into our physical activity and world. We must have balance.

Thank you for that insight, Gloria. I was wondering why a healer would smoke or drink or cuss. We think of our spiritual leaders as *perfect*. I guess, if you were perfect, none of us would ever believe we could aspire to your level. You're right. God is a smart hummer. Also, with you having these same *imperfections* and talking so freely about them helps each of us to stop judging ourselves so badly, which is probably what is healing the addictions and weaknesses, anyway.

Oh, excuse me, Glo-bug, but I'd like to change the subject for a second. What are some of your thoughts about angels? Have you seen one, or talked to one?

Yes, I've seen angels and sometimes they have wings, sometimes they don't. Most of them I've met as I walk through life.

Several weeks ago, our daughter Jaime had seen a program on television about children who see angels. She asked, "Colton, do you ever see angels?" Enunciating clearly, he said, "Yesssss."

"Where have you seen angels, Colton?" He replied, "In my 'Gromma'-who-calls-me-Boo-Boo's bedroom."

"Do they ever talk to you, Colton?" He responded, "Not with their lips." Being reflective he shared further, "But they can't ever leave her room." When Jaime asked why, he clearly stated, "Because they don't have their shoes on."

A week following this discussion, my grandson was going to spend the night with Kirk and me. It was time for bed and Colton and I, as usual, "went to the big bed to hold hands and do love light."

I quietly asked, "Colton, are there any angels in Granny's

bedroom tonight?" "Yesssss . . . just one—right there," and he pointed toward the end of the bed. As our minds melded, he telepathically projected what he was seeing and I could "see" the angel facing us.

"Is she talking to you, Colton?" He moved his lips in an exagerrated way and said, "She's doing this, but no sound is coming out." I asked him to silence his mind and listen to determine whether she was trying to say something to him.

I clairaudiently heard a message and, seeking validation, I asked, "Colton, did she just say she loves you and is watching over you?" Excited (as if he wasn't fully trusting himself either), he remarked, "Oh yes, Gromma, she did."

With his small hand, he pressed his fingers firmly into my cheek, mashing my head into the pillow and said sternly, "Gromma. It's late. It's time to go to sleep. Close your eyes. I'll see you in the morning."

Taking the scolding tone well, I said, "You're right, Colton. I love you. Goodnight. See you in the morning."

Several minutes passed and urgently he tapped my cheek, "Gromma, Gromma . . . wake up." Concerned, I asked, "What, Colton? What's wrong?"

In a sweet, sweet tone, he pointed his index finger and motioned from the end of the bed to the ceiling above us as he replied, "Look, Gromma, she's flying." He said, "The angel just said she's going to sleep up there tonight."

Colton and the appearances of angels have occurred often since then. One evening, he said an angel appeared at the foot of my bed "with a little girl and a little boy who had been burned badly and the angel needed my help for them." Colton hasn't yet learned what "burned very badly" means, knowing nothing about fires, and he doesn't consciously know I'm a healer who helps others.

As a spiritual healer, Gloria, it amazes me that you teach that people should continue with health care professionals. Even you turn to doctors from time to time. I was so surprised to read that in your other writings. Here, you have this beautiful and direct connection to God; yet, you still believe in the medical world.

It always surprises people that I would turn to the medical world when I have this extraordinary gift. Ole Dr. Globug needs to lighten things up and explain why.

A group of people are lined up, waiting to get through the Pearly Gates. St. Peter is checking in each incoming soul just as a guy, in a white doctor's coat, cuts in line and walks straight through the Gates of Heaven. A man, who'd been patiently waiting his turn, asks St. Peter, "Hey. What's the deal here?" St. Peter smiles and says, "Oh, that's just God playing doctor."

I see God appearing in all forms and being in harmony with every outer appearance. Seeing God in a doctor would only have a spiritually good outcome. (No opposition.)

Gloria, you have given me such a gift—this trip, your time and teachings. I would really love to give you something in return. Is there anything special I could do for you?

Yes, actually, there is something you could do for me. Do random acts of kindness toward others. Other than that, I can't think of anything I need. In fact, my friend Nikki and some of my loved ones tell me that I'm hard to buy for "because I have everything." That doesn't mean I live in a fancy house surrounded by treasures or that I have gems up the "wazoo" and that my bank account runneth over. I have love given to me daily, in countless forms.

Name three blessings for me, Gloria, just something that feels special in this moment to you.

I have many things to be grateful for. Hmmm . . . but you're going to limit me to three, huh? First, my grandson thinks the biggest treat at my house "is to get to be with me." (I'm his favorite toy.) Second, our twenty-four-year-old daughter, Jaime, told me she loves to buy me gifts and cards. She reads them all at the counters, and it's so easy to choose one because they easily express her love for me.

Third. Imagine your youngest child, your baby . . . who stands beautifully in support of you every day of your life, believing in you, encouraging you to reach for the stars, and celebrating those successes as if they were her own. Danielle.

Danielle says the words aloud to me all the time, but it's special to receive cards written as if they were personalized.

The last card she gave me referred to the time when I read storybooks and tucked her in at night. She is grateful that I listened to her worries and told her everything would be all right, She says she learned from my example how to be generous and kind . . .

Personally, I don't believe children ever outgrow a mom's sweet love and gentle touch.

Danielle knows she will always be important in somebody's eyes. Because of the confidence I have in her, she believes that her dreams can come true.

In her last mushy card to me, Danielle's sign-off was, "It may not seem like it, at times, that you know what you are doing or that it is actually for the best, but I am always proven wrong. *No regrets.* I am happy for this life you have given me."

Boy. Isn't that the truth? As parents, we don't always know what we're doing—but for a teenager to realize that it's always out of love and concern . . . what a blessing that is.

My son, D.W., will graduate this year. He teases me that he'd like to send me on an exotic cruise, but he knows I would miss him too much.

He recently told me he was planning on joining the marines after he graduates. Oh my God. That just makes me have a stronger desire to get peace on this earth even faster, so he never will have to go to war.

Several years ago, while the Desert Storm conflict was occurring, I'd gotten a call from a church to pray for a local boy, that he would come home safely. I said, "I'll make you a deal. You pray for all the enemies, I'll pray for the boy— and I promise he'll come home safely."

When both D.W. and Danielle told me they wanted to join the services—Danielle wants to become a fighter pilot—I took them to see the movie *Saving Private Ryan* to show them the realities of war. I guess I was hoping it would gross them out or frighten them into a "safe" occupation or dream. As we were leaving the movie theater, in a cocky/smarty-pants tone, I said, "So . . . now that you've seen that movie, I'm sure you'll reconsider."

"Never, Mom, **now more than ever,** we want to join the services." My plan had backfired. I couldn't believe it. They had seen men stumbling on the shores, missing arms and in shock. The wounded and dead were trampled on, and bodies carpeted the shore. Legs missing, endless blood, and total insanity that human beings could do this to one another. I guess the lesson was more for me than my children.

"Mom, we love this country and would be willing to lay down our lives to keep it free and safe. We would think you would be proud of us for that."

I am.

When I read your book and columns years ago, I admit—I got addicted to your beautiful family. I was disappointed when you stopped writing the column. Could you update me on Kerrie and Kirk?

This past summer, the entire family flew to Houston for Kerrie's wedding. She married her handsome knight in shining armor and I swear—she was the most beautiful bride I've ever seen in my entire life. Chiseled beauty. She could have been a model in any bridal magazine. You think I'm just a proud mamma, don't you? I am. But, really, she was so gorgeous; I couldn't even look at her throughout the day and evening reception. Every time I did, I'd cry.

Kerrie works for United Space Alliance in Houston, Texas. Good grief, she became an astronautical/aeronautical engineer. She figures out the jet propulsion for the shuttle missions, and I teased, "Kerrie, why didn't you choose an occupation that had a little stress?" She just finished her thesis for her master's degree, as well. What a kid.

And, Kirk, whew. God, I love that man. He's still working at Smurfit/Stone Container and driving two hours each day. You know, I just decided that I probably shouldn't talk about him right this second or I'm going to get carried away. I can feel it in my bones. . . . He makes every day of my life so special. How do you encapsulate those feelings and experiences in a few short sentences? I'll talk about him bit-by-bit throughout this weekend so it doesn't nauseate you. All the mushy "goo" I feel could also overwhelm you.

Gloria, the Benish clan sounds like a great family. Do you always have such close family ties? How do they feel about your spiritual life and the service you perform as a healer, author, and speaker?

The Benish clan is a great family. Most often, we have "family ties," and sometimes like others in today's society, we find ourselves "untied." Being a peacemaker, I go into total "knots" when we're not all being like the Musketeers, "All for one and one for all." Life is such a process, isn't it? If I didn't have the spiritual experiences (to give me awareness) and the ability to "reconnect" to the Source, at will (to put that awareness into action), I just don't know whether I could handle all that happens in a human's experience on this planet.

Our family of six displays every level in the world concerning spirituality. Kirk lives it, he doesn't have to talk about it or read about it. Kerrie turns to the violet Light, as needed. Jaime is just getting interested and is open-minded to listening. Danielle wants me "to do it for her," and D.W. doesn't want to hear about it. I respect my family's choices. We accept one another.

It's because I know that what I live and teach *works,* that I think every mother in the world should be given an opportunity to have the same awareness on how to help their children and loved ones. ("Oh, sure," I can hear your thoughts. "One *more* thing for *me* to do.") I don't want you to carry the responsibility. I will teach you how to become strong and you can teach your family *how to become strong,* as well. Women, in general and by nature, are nurturing and caring . . . but so many times they deplete themselves, and it's just not necessary. Countless men, of course, do this too.

That, in fact, will be one of my Spokane speeches, so I won't cover that teaching now. I never preplan a speech, but I do get glimpses of what direction the inspiration will go.

I'd love to hear about your life, your family ties, as well. . . .

8
. . . And Untied

For one thing, Gloria, I am in the process of healing myself of co-dependency, the need to be responsible for those who are so irresponsible. I'm also a caretaker. I am at a level of understanding now, to teach my friends and loved ones how to do things for themselves rather than always feeling the responsibility to do everything myself. I hope that this won't offend you, but I have a joke about co-dependency. "How many recovering co-dependents does it take to change a lightbulb? None. They "release it with love," and tell it to go screw itself.

As a little girl, I'd seen enough Walt Disney films and read the Grimm's fantasies often enough that I believed fairy tales could come true. I expected to grow up and live happily-ever-after. Along the way, like others, of kissing a lot of frogs or thinking the beautiful princess would awaken, thinking they would change into the handsome prince or the perfect fairy-tale ending; it didn't happen and I was disappointed. But, I falsely believed that it was *I* who needed to magically transform *them.* I learned the hard way, because I'm such a slow learner, that a frog is a frog and a lazing princess is a lazing princess. I don't have the power to change anyone into anything.

It wasn't until I became aware that I didn't have the ability to turn an alcoholic into a sober, healthy individual or a greedy person into a giving one, that I became more conscious of my co-dependency.

I never liked books or movies that didn't have the happily-ever-after ending. I always read the last chapter of a book first and if it didn't end happily, I didn't waste my time reading it.

Wow. It sounds as if we lived parallel lives. What I just heard could have been my life, as easily. I even avoided movies in which the hero died. Unknowingly, Kirk took me on a romantic get-away weekend. It began with dinner, then a "supposed love story" movie, followed with a suite that had an in-room Jacuzzi.

The movie was *Sommersby* with that ole handsome, hunka/hunka burnin' love, Richard Gere. By the end of the movie I was cussing. Kirk kept "shushing" me, saying, "Gloria, hush. People will hear you."

"I don't care if people hear me—I hated that movie." Had I known the hero would die, I would have never attended the viewing. Although Kirk attempted to make me feel better about "dying for honor," and explaining that the hero had no other choice, I was not consoled. I'll bet you're already aware that the "romantic mood" was gone. Zip. Nada.

Being so frightened my entire life, with pressures of survival and fears of being alone—I stayed in relationships that weren't for my highest good. Some of them became habits, and not necessarily good ones. "De-Nile" is more than just a river in Egypt.

Like you, the fantasies of my childhood and early adulthood never transformed into daily reality. To this day, I still cannot publicly speak of my first marriage. Not that the information wouldn't be helpful, but I don't yet know how to write of those experiences without making the reader dislike my first husband. Not only does he deserve privacy, but also he doesn't deserve to be hated. Those things we experienced together, though uncomfortable, are not for the benefit of a soap opera that could be harmful to him.

Many of the personalized fairy tales I've written in other book forms do express those painful moments and experiences, but spoken in third person . . . or with another character's name attached to the individual situations, which can still continue to teach, but in order to respect a soul's right to privacy.

I know that some fantasies deteriorate quicker than others as the handsome knights change into little children who leave their clothes on the floor, their beer cans on the end tables, and razor stubble (if they even shave) as remnants in the sink for the wives to clean. And what of the knights' dreams of their lovely ladies, whose glass slippers change into scruffy, old worn-out slipper moccasins that get drenched when they carry the last of the trash to the streets' Dumpsters in the rain? And their lovely gowns that transform into jogging suits that cover their aging and ever-so-out-of-shape bodies?

Not that I'm enjoying that you were ever miserable, Gloria, like I and others have been . . . but knowing that you felt all these things and experienced what we have gives men and women hope for better lives.

I've teased before that because my life was so dysfunctional, it would take me many years and countless books to relate just how far one is able to grow. I'd like to share an example of a tale I wrote for one of my books. I feel safe enough with you to share this and to be truthful that this was written concerning myself, rather than a friend, loved one, convict, celebrity, or stranger.

A Drama: The Case of the Missing Identity

The stage and props were set, the curtain went up to expose a drama that blended tragedy, humor, and reality. The time was modern-day, the location was "any city suburb," and the performer was a mom, playing a bit part in a slow-paced movie of life.

The actress had previously played grand roles, in major businesses, but had chosen to quit her career to express motherhood. She had no lines to rehearse before she stepped into the spotlight and she got stage fright, for she was only able to imitate the character through her own mother and friends.

Mom found all stages of her growth in this performance exciting (in the beginning), for it was a new acting career . . . she was able to ad lib or ham things up when the script got too serious.

Mom didn't get raises, there was no further praise for a job well done, there were heavy pressures and deadlines, and she would never receive an Academy Award for her performance. Only years would tell the complete story if "she'd done a good job."

Friends would inquire, "When are you going back to work?" and Mom would teasingly respond that she didn't think she'd ever *stopped* working. She had chosen the hardest role of all to play . . . much more difficult than even she had anticipated, for the hours were long, in fact, never-ending . . . for the dishes were endless and the laundry, too—no matter what, there was always more to do.

She wore many masks: she became a clown, trouper, villain, comedian, pantomimist, and juggler. However, her "makeup" began and ended . . . with the beds.

Mom went on strike against housework, for no matter how much she did, she did not feel appreciated. She allowed things to slide, except for the true matters of importance. (A spider had patiently woven a web in her dining room and it had been there so long . . . surely the spider had long since become senile, forgetting where he'd left it—or long ago died of old age.)

Mom felt she had lost her identity, for she had forgotten WHO SHE WAS by playing so many roles. She was far more than her children's mom and her spouse's wife. She knew this with all her heart but wasn't aware how to express it, and resentment began building.

She was no one's fool. She had plenty to talk about (besides potty training and teething). However, she had been pigeonholed, limited by the beliefs of others that all she'd have to offer a conversation was updates on soap operas or broken-down appliances.

Mom was inspired by people and life's experiences and chose to take an hour a day, away from laundry, cooking, and cleaning, in order to get an important message to the world. She began a daily diary of writings, feeding her innermost, deepest thoughts and feelings into it . . . and it soon became her third creation.

She wrote, not to save a world, not to make money by publishing her ideals, nor to prove her worth to thoughtless, unsupportive friends or family. She wrote . . . because it was what SHE LOVED TO DO (and she was aware that when we do what we love—the money will follow . . . and THE UNIVERSE WILL SUPPORT US).

Mom also knew her writings would assist others in claiming their specialty, disallowing themselves or others to restrict them from finding their own niche.

There is no ending, for the writings are timeless and

each person has equal opportunity "to write their own script." The true beginning was realizing that Mom had to perform for no one but herself. She daily stood upon the worldly stage, in the Light of the Spirit, and had fully released the idea that she had to upstage anyone or try to become a superstar. She didn't have to impersonate anyone and she may never see her name in lights, but she would know that by being who she was, she succeeded by helping to make the lives of others a little brighter. (And, it all began the day she learned to appreciate herself.)

No offense, please, to what I'm about to say. I'm not a feminist—I love being treated like a lady, and I respect men for all they do and who they are. But I have to say that I thought about it a lot and I think it would be wonderful if a housewife/mother ran the country. It would be budgeted and in balance. She'd know where everything was and how to solve every conflict of *neighboring/fighting children.* The *children of the world* would learn how to pick up after themselves, how to share (because there's plenty for everyone); they would learn manners and how to respect themselves, as well as others. They would learn pride and honor, for in being part of a loving and healthy (spiritual) family, all members would do their share or forfeit their allowance. They would learn from their mother, rather than from a paid teacher, what is and isn't appropriate. Most of all, they would learn to be *a team.* Mothers have the power, not schools, not heads of states, but the housewife/mother who, as an expression of love, does this and more. *Usually, all in one day.*

Amen. You certainly bring home the importance of motherhood, Glo-bug.

Being a mother of four doesn't make me an authority by any means. I wanted to raise healthy-minded children whom I could release into society and who would add strength to our nation, rather than being a burden to it. I spent years teaching them manners and giving them wholesome guidelines to follow. I encouraged each of them to dream big.

I was mocked by friends, I embarrassed my children, and as a "Princess Bride," I was probably a "royal pain in the ass" to my first husband.

Gloria, as concerned parents, we . . . the dads and moms, all of us people in the world, could wonder and judge how the moral fabric of our society has been damaged and whether there's hope for it to be mended. We baby boomers can look back to our programming as children of *Father Knows Best, Leave It to Beaver,* and *The Brady Bunch.* Although they were sweet sitcoms, and problems could be resolved in thirty minutes (minus commercial time), they weren't realistic. I teased for years that I was a family member of "June Cleaver's clan," but I didn't get paid for my acting.

Today's children have heroes who belch and fluffy (pass gas), and though the sense and tones of humor have changed—they are being imprinted with unrealistic values just as we were. Neither the overly positive nor the crude and rude negative messages are the answer to resolve the world's issues or our individual needs.

Wholesome and helpful entertainment can be a reality, but unfortunately, not at our present state of awareness. To name but a few examples, a U.S. president can lie under oath and not suffer penalty from perjury. Our political parties spend their time in office preplotting and planning *consciously* how to destroy the next term of officers (which affects all of us, keeping us in conflict with one another, rather than working together as a whole team to do what's best for our country.) Our federal buildings can be bombed and our children shot in schools.

We, the people of this world, look at these situations and feel helpless and hopeless to do anything to change them. We look at our individual lives and feel helpless and discouraged. We deal daily with our behavior, the behavior of our children and mates, the bills, depression, and prices that continue to escalate. God help us.

As concerned, caring, compassionate (and many times, co-dependent) souls, we think we're doing good just to get through a day without some form of crisis. It's enough if someone didn't hurt our feelings or offend us in some way. We become closet drinkers or find other addictions to numb us just to get through everyday situations and tasks. We've lost our sense of direction and purpose. We feel guilty that our roles as housewives and mothers . . . or fathers, and society as a whole, are not fulfilling, and we fear anyone knowing how resentful we are becoming. We want excitement in our lives. God, we just want to feel alive again.

How is it, though, that we can do anything to "fix" the bigger picture when we have presented tunnel vision and can't even think of what to fix for dinner tonight?

I can understand so easily. Do I need to remind you how severely depressed I was fifteen years ago when I wrote that fairy tale? My first husband thought I was dying. I was willing myself to do so. If this was "fun," then I'd definitely had enough.

In answer to your question, this is how I'd like to respond. My daughter Jaime came to me after she'd had Colton and said, "Mom, I need to lose fifty pounds." Immediately I remarked, "You'll never be able to do it, Jaime."

Shocked by my response, she cried, "What do you mean

I'll never do it? You, of all people, are always so positive—how can you doom me to not succeeding?"

I wasn't giving Jaime a doom or gloom failure report. I was offering valid wisdom from experience. "You can't lose fifty pounds, Jaime. If you try, you will fail." I continued, "Fifty pounds is so much to lose, you'll unconsciously sabotage your efforts. You'll be overwhelmed before you even begin.

"Set short-term goals, Jaime. In reality, you only have to lose one pound. Once you achieve that goal, knowing you can accomplish that, you'll be able to lose another pound, and another, and another."

Jaime reached her goal, dropping several dress sizes. She lost weight and inches, and gained in self-respect, esteem, and confidence. She feels beautiful and good about herself and indeed, she is beautiful . . . now that she's good to herself.

Finding peace within us and our hearts and homes will be what "fixes" those bigger problems. Loving ourselves is not vain or self-centered. It is necessary and I give you full permission to put yourself first. I encourage you to do it immediately.

Most of us, the majority in fact, don't know how to love ourselves or even begin. Here are ways to get started, even on a superficial level:

1. A "Calgon-take-me-away" bath.
2. A manicure.
3. A pedicure.
4. A day at the beauty shop or local spa.
5. A day window shopping (because you can't afford to buy for you. The kids need shoes, school projects, field trips, band instruments, a "required" calculator for algebra that costs $100, etc.)

6. An afternoon curled up on the sofa with an international tea and a good book (without interruptions . . . which, of course, are the key words here).

7. A variety of other false and fleeting attempts to make ourselves feel good.

For men, treats for themselves may include:

1. A day at their favorite football game.

2. Mountain climbing, hiking, panning for gold in a cool stream of water.

3. Surfing the Web sites (without ten thousand questions and interruptions from wife and kids).

4. A romantic weekend and "getting lucky."

5. Being a couch potato and channel surfing.

6. Tinkering in the garage.

7. Getting a night out with the boys, getting lit, without a "guilt trip" later.

I think, NOW IS THE TIME to learn how to love yourself. In every speech I make and in every book I'm fortunate to get into print, I'll continue to share examples of how to achieve healing for these major issues of our lives. As we unite in (Divine) purpose, we'll no longer be "fit to be tied," we'll be able to enjoy those family ties after all. . . .

9

Do You Want to
Be Right, or Be Happy?

We're nearing our exit here in Coeur d'Alene, to have
lunch, so I'd like to share some random ideas with you.
First of all, I hope I won't offend your religious beliefs
about "the devil," because everyone has a right to his or her
own beliefs, limitations, and fears. But, if you wouldn't
mind, I'd like to express reality, from my perception.

**I'd love to hear your ideas about that subject, Gloria. I
never believed in Satan either, but I couldn't understand
how, if there wasn't a devil, we could experience so much
ugliness in this world.**

Many years ago, my brother-in-law Chuck, in listening to
my experiences, believed that one day I would meet Satan
face to face. He has a strong Southern Baptist background
and believes that the closer one gets to God, the more one
becomes tempted and swayed from the path of Light.
Because I had so many direct experiences with God, Chuck
believed that I would meet the devil.

I never believed God made a force in opposition to
Himself. Imagine my surprise, then, when one evening as I

lay down to go to sleep, I closed my eyes—my inner vision opened and the Hollywood version of Satan stood upon a lighted stage.

With a strong, sucking action, I felt like I was being pulled toward him. I resisted. I felt extraordinary fear. Total terror, in fact. The energy field was getting stronger and stronger and I didn't think I had enough strength within me not to get sucked in.

Aha. Then I realized, "Oh yeah, I don't even believe in you. In fact, you're nothing. God didn't create you; therefore, you have no reality." The image of Satan dissolved.

It was then that I understood, more than ever, "why" I can be used as an instrument for Spirit to perform healings. Cancer, AIDS, and other diseases don't scare me. God didn't create them; therefore, they have no reality in His mind. Since I am One with and in His mind, my consciousness disbelieves in the existence of a force separate or in opposition to the One Power. Cancer and AIDS dissolve just like the image/illusion of Satan in the vision of that night.

That's all well and good, when you're lying down and purposefully allowing yourself to be used as an instrument for the Divine—but what do you do when you're going through your day-to-day experiences and run across negativity?

Personally, I have to ask myself, "Do I want to be right or be happy?" If I choose to be right, I have the right to create conflict . . . powers in opposition. It's not as much fun now that I'm aware, though.

Please explain.

We all have an ego, and I have been a person who always "likes to get the last word in." I was never good at arguing because I would freeze up and didn't have any thoughts or good "come-backs" to snap off my tongue toward another. I was terrified of confrontation. (Nikki is the one who taught me that I was safe enough to express my "opinion.")

It seemed as if God didn't give me very good tools to argue with. I've had to develop that as a part of my nature. Unfortunately, the only classes that teach us how to do that are life itself, and the raising of our awareness. As that occurs, our fears of those situations dissolve and we find we don't experience them any longer.

Another parallel. I've always admired people who could "just say it the way it is," except if it was directed toward me, of course. I thought they must be so secure, within themselves, to not fear verbal, emotional, or a physical attack. For most of my life, I've felt weak and hated myself because of it. I really needed this weekend retreat.

I prefer to be happy for the majority of the time, which doesn't mean I'm sacrificing ideals or integrity. We don't have to sacrifice in order to be in harmony with people, places, and things. We meet opposition and silently realize, "I am in harmony with this situation," and we watch as both people ARE in harmony, but without ego's battling or humanly attempting to "make it happen."

When we raise our consciousness to the state of harmony, Divine and miraculous things begin happening through us. Remember. The violet Light is that state of awareness.

In the beginning, God created All That Is, and He looked upon it and called it "Good." (Not good and bad. A repeat, I know, but a necessary one.) Those things that appear "bad" in the human experience are the "illusions" held in the mind of man. In the Bible it says, "Resist not evil."

For just a moment think of God as being all Life. The word "live," then, when spelled backwards is "evil." A force in opposition. When we no longer resist those appearances of evil, but find ourselves in harmony with them, the "illusion" of the appearance changes to that which God created. Our individual minds are healed, and our lives mirror the inner changes.

As an example, two years ago, my parents celebrated their fiftieth wedding anniversary. My dad had secretly called me to officiate and renew their vows. The original best man and maid of honor were being flown in from Alaska, to Denver, for the celebration. Friends and loved ones from near and far were arriving. My mom was aware of the party, but the renewal of vows was a secret until the last moment. I wrote and read a personalized fairy tale for my parents, coming from my dad, to my mother, entitled, "I'd Do It all Again with You."

Following the renewing of vows, the guests celebrated. It was a beautiful day for everyone involved. I had three beers that night, and I'd never, probably, had three beers in an entire year . . . let alone within a few hours' time. I was lit. Talk about glowing.

After the guests left, I found myself sitting with my elbows propped on the table and my fingers trying to hold my eyes open. I was surprised that my speech wasn't slurred, but trying to keep my eyes open was impossible. I went and lay upon my sister's waterbed and whew! The room started spinning and I thought I was going to barf.

I immediately realized that *I had created a power in opposition with God, concerning the alcohol.* Lying in the dark and closing my eyes and feeling the spinning, I silently said, "I am One with God Who constitutes my Oneness with all spiritual beings, ideas, and creations . . . including the alcohol I drank." I was immediately sober. I was in harmony with the alcohol—no longer in opposition.

I use this truth in everyday situations and find my individual life "in the flow" with the One Life. I am in harmony with the food I eat, the medication I take, the cigarettes I smoke, and every word that flows forth from my pen. I am One with All That Is . . . Therefore, unless I make the separation, I don't experience duality. No good *and* bad! I experience spiritual good by being in harmony (which has no opposite experience).

Again, it's so refreshing to know that even you experience the realities of this dimension, Gloria. I can imagine you are judged for this behavior, though. Not only "shouldn't you drink," but also you drank more "than was necessary," and "you, of all people, should KNOW BETTER." Yet, you seem to do this purposefully to place yourself in our positions of learning, growing, and experiencing life. You do it to teach us how to surrender our judgments of all those things we've been taught that we're bad if we do.

Oh, and personally, I like my teacher to be able to say, "Been there/done that," rather than one who professes to do good and behind my back, does the opposite. You could "hide" this human side from us and no one would be the wiser, but you openly admit everything that can help others. You'll face more judgments, of course, from the masses, perhaps, but I, for one, am grateful you're willing to share all this.

"Wow. Talk about getting carried away and "getting up on a soap box." Sorry. Where is Spirit guiding you to speak to me now?

The paint was peeling from the top of my van, in six-inch sheets. My warranty was about to expire and I made an appointment. Together, Kirk and I drove the three hours to the company where I had purchased the vehicle. As we pulled up to the parts department, Kirk said, "Okay, Gloria, go work your magic so we don't have to pay for this out-ofpocket. Do whatever it is that makes people want to bend over backward to give you whatever you want."

I was shocked. "Kirk, what I do isn't magic—and I'm not even going to get out of this car, unless you realize that I am One with the van, the car company, the paint, and everything that touches this experience." I continued, "You must understand that I never manipulate people . . . I live the Truth and would never do unto another what I wouldn't be willing to have done unto me."

Kirk smiled and said, "Okay, Gloria, okay . . . whatever you say—but, I'm telling you—if the company doesn't pay to have this van repainted, it's going to cost us at least $1,000."

"Kirk, if we have to come up with the $1,000, it will be available before we know we need it. We **always** have everything we need, usually before we know we need it."

"Whatever," he replied.

The manager came out to look at our van and brought a camera to take photos of the peeling paint. He remarked, "Of course this will be covered under warranty," and Kirk and I were given three sets of tickets to newly released movies, free tickets for a gondola ride, complimentary rides to breakfast, and an offer of a free bar-be-que lunch held at the car company.

You see, I was in harmony with the car company. I wasn't trying to "pull anything over on anyone" or "take advantage." I was One with them, and whatever I was doing to them, I was doing to an aspect of myself.

My life works (on all levels).

Gloria, even as I hear these words, my mind wanders to the many situations I've encountered recently and throughout my life, in which this information would have come in very handy. But because it's easier to remember spiritual

principles, or life-saving tips as you call them, through stories, this information will be easier to draw upon as I continue to grow. In fact, even at present, I'm going through a
rough time with a few friendships. It's easier to place
blame on another than to believe I had anything to do
with the problem. All your relationships are probably always loving and perfect, right?

In my forty-seven years of life, I had an opportunity to
meet seven people I didn't like. Oh yeah . . . make that
eight. Anyway, actually, I liked them in the beginning—and
when they didn't like me, I tried various ways to "make
them like me." When I couldn't find a way to manipulate
them into liking me . . . the next best thing was not to
like them, in return. When I became spiritual at age thirty-
two, I realized, however, I was willing to allow God to love
them through me.

The reason I just added number eight to my list is because of a dear friend who decided she "didn't want to play
with me anymore." She gave me two feeble reasons "why"
and I kept trying to get her "to clean it up" with me, because
there had to be more reasons why she didn't want to write
or call me.

I was never very good at rejection and I couldn't understand her decision. Why was she withholding love from
me? It didn't make any sense to me. We had such deep love
for each other and I couldn't believe that something so trivial (if she was being honest), could end a relationship. Of
course, it wasn't "trivial" to her—I had pushed one of her
"buttons," and she wasn't willing to discuss the issue. I had
severely hurt her, unintentionally.

She asked me to respect her wishes. I did. I also prayed
and asked, "Forgive her Father, for she knows not what she's
doing." She, of course, had "set the karmic law into mo-

tion," and someone would withhold love, in some form, from her.

Each time I would think about her (or was she thinking of me, since I'm telepathic?)—I would send a silent, "I am in harmony with your decision." She may (or may not) return as a daytime friend, but I am no longer losing sleep (or power) over her decision.

Daily, the perfect love and peace is felt because I am in harmony with everyone and everything that touches my mind, body, and experience. When I sense "opposition" in the forms of pain (emotional or physical), human disagreements, or "not getting what I want," I remind myself that I have turned the word L - I - V - E into E - V - I - L . . . it is I who have created a power and sense of separation from God. The mirror of my mind and what I falsely believe can be retranslated in a holy moment, back into His Divine image, once we are aware.

I believe the following story will help teach you a very important lesson in understanding joy, as well as abundance in all things in your life.

I was invited to a spiritual gathering in a neighboring state where I would renew friendship ties with countless people who had been the wind beneath my wings, supporting me and helping me to help others. Among the participants there was a group of vendors with beautiful clothing, books, and spiritual tools for self-awareness.

As the day's event opened, the group joined hands and a prayer was said, giving thanks for the abundance that would come to each. My heart thudded. I wanted to offer a few words to the group, but as an invited guest, I remained silent. Those who came "to get" were disappointed that the public didn't attend and "support them."

The following day, I attended another local spiritual gathering and I paid the fee to attend. Instead of getting to enjoy the people and their booths, I found myself "in a closet," doing private healings. Once it was discovered I was available, people lined up. I laughed about my "office," because it had been six years ago—in this very building—that I went "public," and "was brought out of the closet." Years later, I was a "closet spiritual healer" again.

I was asked to participate in a raffle and I said, "I'm probably going to win and I could do that with purchasing one ticket, but this is such a good cause, I'll buy five." Of course I won. The money from admission fees, along with the raffle, would be used to help local families during the holidays, assisting with meals and gifts for their children.

Although I was an invited guest and wouldn't have had to pay to attend, I didn't go to this gathering "to get"; I went to give. Three of those I healed that day offered to donate to me. Intuitively I knew these people always give, therefore, I wanted to give them an opportunity just to receive.

An 85-year-old woman, who had driven downtown from the farthest point of the city "just to see me" offered to donate. I said, "Hannah, my goodness, I am so fulfilled and filled full . . . I have so much to give, please allow me to do so. Infinite love flows through me—please, just receive it."

I've said it before and I'll say it again and again. Abundance isn't in how much you receive; it's in how much you have to give. If you're trying to get it, you will experience lack and frustration. Once you realize that you already "have it," and its infinite nature, through your giving (or mere intention to give) unlimited opportunities of experiencing abundance on all levels will open to you.

I have so much to be thankful for, but most of all, my gratitude is for this simple awareness. I hope this vital secret will teach you how to be happy as well.

Do I want to be right or be happy? Usually happy, but it just depends on the mood I'm in. There's nothing wrong with choosing to be a human and experiencing the human scene, but I believe it's important to at least be aware that you have a choice.

Don't tell me. A day comes when we realize we can actually be BOTH?

Yup. Oh, here's the restaurant. Please feel free to order anything you wish—and please don't look at the prices. During this journey, I'd like to ask you to raise your standards. Choose those things you have always wanted to eat, but couldn't afford. Choose the experiences you'd wish to have. Say those things you've been afraid to say. Feel the emotions you've wanted to express. In fact, you don't have to answer me on this one—take some time to think about it—but what could and would you do, if you just trusted that you wouldn't fail?

Now that I've told you (coming from my awareness of abundance and possibilities) what you can ask of me or expect from the universal unlimited, infinite possibilities, every day of your life, are you beginning to feel like a Happy Hummer, too?

Join me—a feast of life awaits us.

10

Spiritual (Daily) Bread Crumbs . . . Loving Morsels to Follow if You've Lost Your Way

Before you begin eating, I encourage you to perform a simple exercise. Remember how rubbing your hands together and placing them on a pained area can heal it? I want you to rub your hands together and place them approximately an inch or two above your food. I normally never say "grace" at meals, aloud anyway, but I do ask God to bless my food and I give thanks for the loving hands that prepared it for me.

Blessing means "purification." Blessing your food dissolves the anger or emotions that someone was carrying while growing, packaging, or preparing your food. Everything is energy, and think, merely, how another can sometimes influence your attitude. You might be flyin' the friendly skies and meet "Mr. Bummer of an attitude," and you can easily be brought down to his level. Food, clothing, pets, and so forth can take on the energy of the environment and emotional energy from individuals.

By placing your hands above the food, you may feel an erratic type of energy. If you aren't sensing anything in this particular situation, the next time you go to your local grocery store, try this experiment. In the aisle of beans—pinto, navy, or any variety—see how erratic the energy feels. Rub your hands together and place them over the unopened package. Sharp, Mexican–jumping bean sensations will prickle the palm of your hand. With your hands in this position for even a few minutes, you'll begin to feel a peaceful sense of energy in this food group. (Ha. And you wondered why you became a motorboat after eating beans?)

You only need to have your hands over your food for a few seconds, and you will know that the food will maintain and sustain you, and your body will be in harmony with the meal. Amazing, isn't it? Simply amazing.

Dr. Glo-bug, I am in awe of how you do, literally, incorporate spirituality into every detail of your life. All this spiritual food for thought today is so delicious to all my senses. But, even getting such an up close and personal experience with you, I wonder if I'll ever be able to incorporate all this as effectively into my life. Did you learn all this through reading books and going to seminars, or was it all through experience?

Concerning my spiritual path, my greatest sense of accomplishment is that people can read, understand, and incorporate the teachings I have to share. I've attempted to read books for enlightenment but wasn't allowed to. Whether my attention span is shorter than a tsetse fly's "peeper" . . . the books couldn't hold my attention and I would do an "outta body—back in ten minutes" sort of thing. I trusted that Spirit didn't want me to "borrow" someone else's information and attempt to incorporate it into mine. My teachings were to come from direct experiences, and since I'm so "dense" sometimes, if I could understand it . . . anyone could.

As far as your concern whether you can incorporate these life-saving tips, don't think you have to do it all at once. The teachings are for your awareness. You don't need to stress yourself out or think, "you're not doing it right" if you don't do it my way. Be comfortable that your growth is gradual. And I'm always there for others, as needed. I teasingly tell people, "Try it first—and if it doesn't work . . . then call." If someone calls with a life-threatening illness, I don't say, "Go buy my book and do it yourself." I put their name on my prayer list and begin immediately loving them across the miles.

A retired woman, Eleanor, had read my simple guide to self-healing and received a call from her sister Katherine one afternoon. Katherine had been out shopping and had fallen. She had knocked herself silly and was rushed to the emergency room. Tests showed that she didn't have a concussion, but they released her without pain medication and her head hurt severely.

Katherine called Eleanor and asked, "Would you call Gloria and ask if she would pray for me?" Eleanor assured her sister she would. However, as she hung up, she thought, "I've read the book. I'll try it first and then if it doesn't work, I'll call Gloria."

Eleanor's sister hadn't told her which side of the head she'd hurt, but she realized her Oneness with her sister, and scanned her own head, feeling a hotter energy on the above right side. She laid hands upon herself, as taught in *Go Within or Go Without,* and as she finished the thirty minutes of hand placements, she called Katherine to check on her, concerned for her safety.

As they reconnected, Katherine remarked, "Thank you for calling Gloria. Thirty minutes after I called you—my head doesn't hurt any more. Funny thing though, for the entire time, it felt like someone was standing right behind me, working on me." Eleanor, in her first attempt (at healing, and especially, across the miles), proudly said, "I didn't call Gloria. I did it myself."

Gloria, why am I welling up with tears? I feel a knot in my throat from holding it back. It was a nice story, but it wasn't that emotional for me that I would need to cry. As I think of it, as you've been talking today, I felt my eyes tear from time to time.

We cry and can't help it when we feel the Presence of God, whether it's an AT&T commercial, a loving card, a sentiment, or a modern-day miracle.

Take a nice, deep breath, and enjoy your coffee and dessert. I'll just keep sharing more until we leave and finish the last leg of our journey this afternoon.

Four years ago, a university newspaper heard about the man who was healed of AIDS through me and called for an interview. I was asked how Terry had contracted the virus and I replied, "I never asked. I didn't think it was any of my business." The interviewer then asked what his last name is and I replied, "I don't think that's any of *your* business."

Following this interview, I was invited to listen to Terry as he spoke to the Hellgate High School kids in Missoula, Montana. After he recovered, he chose to speak to high school kids across Montana, concerning AIDS awareness, and had asked me to join the afternoon class. I was thrilled to do so.

Since I didn't know any of the facts associated with his illness, I was mesmerized as I listened to his life story. The only thing his cousin Cheryl had told me about Terry was that a person is HIV until the T-cell count drops below 50; then they are classified with the AIDS virus. When I met Terry, his T-cell count was 8.

He spoke of the various stages he'd gone through as well

as the suicides of three of his friends. From the first moment he was told of the virus, he was given a death sentence—not only from the doctor, but also from his friends and family. His friends, one by one, did die.

Terry stood before the teenagers that day, explaining that his cousin encouraged him to come see me, four years ago. He explained to Cheryl that he couldn't possibly make the thirty-minute journey to my home. She replied, "That's too bad, because I already made your appointment." Terry told the kids that it was the most difficult thing he ever did. For one, he didn't have the physical strength to do it, and second, *he didn't believe.*

Not until Terry met me, had he had support in living and overcoming this condition. He mentioned my name, only briefly, in his dialogue. He told the kids, "When I went to see Gloria, I'm sure she didn't know anything about AIDS. But to her, it didn't matter. She just put her arms around me and loved me unconditionally. A few days following the healing, I started to feel stronger. I went back to her again and she loved me again. I felt even stronger."

This part of his speech touched my heart as he said, "Now I just cross my arms over my own chest and love myself as much as Gloria did."

Love healed Terry. I gave him a "life sentence" rather than a death sentence. He was given permission to be himself and have the virus, but to live fully in spite of it. His healing came from within himself, through acceptance. He felt God's love for him, through me. I just loved him with my whole, great big heart until he could love himself as much.

I was so proud of Terry, watching him speak truthfully to teenagers of his guilt, shame, fear, and courageously sharing experiences, "mistakes," and feelings. (Those mistakes were the tools/blessings in disguise to get him where he is today.) His lifestyle, in the fast lane, changed—not from human effort, but naturally, through healing his fears.

Those kids listened to Terry because he was honest about his drugs, sexual escapades, and the huge amounts of money he'd made. He touched their hearts. Terry gave them a safe place to come when they have concerns and questions.

What a wonderful experience and story, Glo-bug. I know several people who have AIDS and I'm willing to learn and teach your technique to as many as I can. I can also think of many other areas where I could help make this information available to family, friends, health care professionals, and my gosh, all of a sudden I feel like I'm on a mission. Maybe this is part of my purpose. I won't dwell on it, but I'll ponder it and listen to my heart. I just get so excited to think of cancer centers, for children and adults, or the many needed areas where this information could be placed.

I know. I've been a healer for sixteen years and a public speaker for ten years—and still, I hadn't even touched the tip of the iceberg. No matter where I go, there is always someone willingly awaiting a helping hand.

I'm thinking, Gloria, but still listening. Continue.

While performing healings in the Pacific Northwest, I met a man who had some severe health conditions. At age forty-six, he suffered a massive heart attack, followed with quadruple bypass surgery. While recovering in the hospital, he had a stroke. A year later, another stroke followed. Over the years, he had been involved in car and motorcycle accidents.

When he arrived for his healing, it took him at least five minutes to travel from the car to the front door. He walked with a limp. It was difficult to get him out of the living room chair and into my healing chair.

He had never been to a healer before; so in preparation, I was explaining some of the feelings he might expect. I told him that some people begin crying immediately because they feel such tremendous love flowing through them. Teasingly I said, "Some people feel so relaxed they fall asleep; so if you start snoring, I won't take offense."

He sat in my canvas-backed healing chair. I rubbed my hands and placed them on top of his head. I silently prayed, **"I trust the Christ within will go forth and perform the greater works."** Immediately following, the violet Light appeared in my inner vision. The gentleman's head *ker-thunked* back against my chest and he began snoring (within milliseconds of me laying hands upon him).

I thought he was teasing and I looked around to his face and truly—he *was* asleep.

He had approximately eight "electrocutions," which jarred him quite strongly in the chair, but he never awoke throughout the healing. Twenty minutes later, I was complete, as guided by Spirit. He awakened, stood, and had *no pain* in his body.

Since you're having a second cup of coffee, I'll just keep telling you another story. I just never run out, do I?

Gary found an outdated flyer, from a workshop, in his area and phoned me. When he arrived in Montana for his healing, he explained his situation. In 1992 he worked for an electric company. Through a miscalculation of human error, 2,500 volts of electricity hit him. The voltage killed him "graveyard dead," but a second jolt restarted his heart. Three days later, he awoke in a hospital with his mother at his side. His first words, "The S - O - Bs didn't get me, did they?" To this day, he didn't know whom he was referring to.

When the electricity exited Gary's body, it blew the back lower part of his head away, along with the right side of his face. It blasted its ferocious power out the lower part of his spine and a place on each leg. He refused morphine or other strong medications, fearing he would become addicted during the reconstructive phases of surgeries. Since 1992 Gary had known daily pain.

"When I awoke, I had the strongest desire and passion to heal people. However, not knowing how to heal even myself, how could I ever possibly hope to help others? That is. . . ," he said, "Until I heard about you, Gloria." Gary went on to say, "I want to learn everything you can possibly teach me, because I will be going to burn units to teach and help others."

Forty minutes after I began channeling the healing energy, Gary walked out of my home—not only without pain, but without a cane. He was literally swinging his cane, remarking that he felt silly even carrying it now since he no longer needed it. (I mentioned to Kirk, how my neighbors must respond seeing people with wheelchairs, crutches, or canes coming in and leaving my home, carrying the tools that once supported them.)

Others seek validation that I can do (or be part of) these miraculous things. They want letters from the medical world supporting Terry's cure from AIDS, and others to "see it in written form" that the things I tell you are true. I respect the privacy of others and don't feel the need to have their lives become as public as mine. If there are those who choose to share their miracles with the public, they can send their "testimonials" to the publisher of this book, for future "validation," if they choose to. But it's not my desire to have these proofs to teach, write, or share my life and experiences. I'm far beyond the need of having to convince anyone of anything. I just do what I do, as matter-of-factly as you arise, brush your teeth, get dressed, and go about your daily routines.

There's something I'd like you to hear. I'm quoting from a letter from my best friend, Nikki. She wrote it for one of my monthly "Helping Hand" columns years ago, but I never forgot it. (I was a spiritual columnist for four years in LuAnn Stallcop's *Open Line* newspaper, teaching her readers those things I'm sharing with you.) Sometimes when I feel I'm not doing enough to help others, I think about Nikki's perception of me and know that I need to take a "chill pill" because I have made a difference.

In this time of confusion and chaos, the once intangible fabric that is God has become more solid than the body of His Son ever was. There lives a child loved by Him. She exists in and for His Light. She bubbles through the lives of the confused and fearful, presenting with laughter and touch the forgotten memory of their true form, power, and connection to the Creator's perfection.

In her forty-plus-four years of this life, Gloria has fed on being and on not being loved by all who've passed her way. Each life in her life became a sure and steady pathway stone furthering her quest to reflect the love so freely given by God to all. A love easily seen and felt by Gloria. A love she discovered early, not so easily accessed by every heart she met.

Gloria was given gifts along the way. She could see and hear God clearly through all of her senses. She began to be aware of healing occurring for herself and others through a touch, a word, a thought. She saw clearly that the layers of awareness leading to the center of God were more numerable than those of an onion . . . some falling away easily, some with tears. In her growing knowledge and gifts, Gloria became the teacher.

Gloria, with love and respect, acknowledged that her journey to the Center was made possible by what she learned from those she taught. She believed they, too, were the voice of God. She reached out and gently escorted any along who wished to travel her way. I, for one, am forever grateful that she held out her soft and tiny hand for me to grasp. Because she could, my hand will forever be held out to others who reach for the Light.

As one who loves her and watches her grow in every aspect and dimension of her life, I can see that Gloria is destined to be counted among the unicorns. Her rareness and uniqueness will be mythological only in the sense that, right now, in this time, she is what she is among so few of her like. We'll remember her as a beginning to what we are all becoming. "One in the heart and mind of God." (Linda K. Fudge 9/2/97)

How wonderful, Gloria. Nikki is a great writer too. She can illustrate through drawings or the written word. Also, I know you're willing to teach others, and me, everything you know, to make our lives the best they can be. How will I ever reach you after this weekend? Through books, of course, but this is the computer age. Do you have a Web site and have you ever thought of having a chat room?

Yes, I do have a Web site: www.miraclehealing.org. I will have continual updates of my spiritual growth, as well as a chat room. I am also including a page that will tell you where I'll be speaking and when. When I'm in your area, maybe we can get together and play again. I want to be available to those who need a little extra love, wisdom, spiritual advice, or just a smile. (Because you just never know what's going to fall out of my mouth, huh?)

That's what I think is so fun about you, Glo-bug. Just when you least expect it, you throw a zinger in. You make life fun. And thank you so much for the lunch, it was simply delicious. And had I looked at the price before I or-

dered it, I might not have done so. I feel proud of myself that I am willing to accept what I really want. Normally, that would have embarrassed me, but it's beginning to feel so right. I am having a great time.

Well, thanks. Are you ready to go then? If you liked this, wait until I show you the room I have reserved for you. You deserve only the best, and you deserve to have it all. This is your life. You are the priority. I'm so glad you're willing to receive, since you've given your entire life.

11

Be an Outlet for Love

Being back in the van, passing this school and seeing the little children, reminds me of a story that I feel is important to share.

I see God in all things and all experiences. God is everywhere present. So is electricity, but it you don't plug into it, you can't enjoy the benefits of it. Plug into the Divine, and become an outlet for love.

The last time I drove my kids to school, my attention was drawn to two strangers, approximately ten and eight years old. The eight-year-old was having trouble walking and I watched as she dragged her right foot behind, unable to lift it. I noticed also that her sister was becoming very annoyed with her. I supposed that it was because her sister felt helpless, worried that they would be late for school.

I continued toward the second block, looking in my rearview mirror to see if the situation would change. It didn't and I flipped a U-turn and returned to the children. I pulled my van alongside the girls and asked if they were okay. The ten-year-old (later introducing herself as Tammi) responded that her sister, Hannah, had broken a blister on her heel. Blood was streaming down the back of her heel and tears filled her eyes.

I asked the girls if they would like a ride to the school, but the offer was rejected. I'm sure they'd been forewarned about getting into a car with a stranger. I encouraged them to accept the ride, knowing it would take Hannah forever to get to school in her condition, along with added, unnecessary pain. Tammi, fortunately, recognized my daughter Danielle in the vehicle, and accepted.

As I drove to the school, I could barely contain my tears as I made simple conversation with the sisters. Each time I turned to look at Hannah and saw her alligator tears, my throat tightened with tears, as well. I dropped my children at the corner and drove Tammi and Hannah as close to the school as I could, to avoid further pain for Hannah. As they exited the van, both children gave me a sincere thank you.

I watched as Hannah dragged her foot, and I sat in front of the school with tears streaming down my face. I wanted so badly to sit her down and lay hands on, but what gives me the right? I hoped that the random act of kindness, generated by love, had been enough to give her the ability to get to the school nurse's office to take care of the situation.

As I drove home with the lump in my throat and continued tears, I thought of sharing this situation in book form. It's a simple experience that each of us encounters in our lives, concerning not only ourselves, but also our children. What makes it so special that I'd devote so much attention to it?

I didn't tell this story to make you think I'm a nice person. The act of love is showing forth the demonstration of God in my life. Love is expressing Itself. I just happen to be the vehicle through which It passes. I feel the Presence of God in every loving gesture, whether it is in the form of a miracle that transcends illness, lack of prosperity, limitation, pain, or fear in any form.

I don't share random acts of kindness in my books to make you like me. I personally don't care if people like me or not, for I'm not seeking the world's approval. My service and deep desire is that you become aware, when you're around me or reading my books. If you feel love emanating from me or from my words, my desire is that you become aware that you are feeling the Individualized Presence of the Divine.

Gloria, I have only known you a short time and yet I feel like I've known you forever. It's so obvious that you don't boast of the miracles that happen through you in order to be looked upon as special or chosen, nor to feed your ego. I can tell that you would be just as content to live a totally silent life, if that was what Spirit asked of you. But through your sharing, you are giving each of us an opportunity to receive a modern-day understanding of an age-old mystery.

Also, knowing what I know now about you, you didn't have the ability to ignore the situation that day, nor others that become part of your experience each day. With your illustrations, I now realize that once I awaken and invite the consciousness of God into my mind, I know and trust that the Presence will go before me and prepare my day. And here I thought I wouldn't understand! Now, in each situation I find my attention drawn to, I will trust my thoughts and take physical action to do what I'm being asked and am fully capable to do.

Wow. I felt the truth in your words. God was speaking through you just then. I could feel the authority of which you spoke.

When I was flying back to Rhode Island last year to teach a workshop, I found myself teaching and healing as we flew the friendly skies. A gentleman from Great Falls, Montana, who sat next to me, listened intently as I talked faster than a speeding bullet. Halfway through our flight, I couldn't stand it any longer and said, "Todd, I'm feeling the pain in your neck and it's just about to kill me."

He affirmed that he's always had the pain and went on to explain the constant migraines he gets from it.

"Would you mind very much if I touch you to show you exactly where the energy is blocked?" He gave permission and I reached up to touch it. Instantaneously as my fingers came into contact with his neck, the pain dissolved. I rotated my neck and said, "Thanks for not hurting me any more." Todd explained that his neck had hurt for fourteen years. Almost apologetic, I replied, "Well, it doesn't hurt any more. . . ."

Todd was impressed. (So was I.) In a realization of Oneness, there weren't two necks, his and mine. There was only one. When I no longer feel the pain, neither does the other person. Remember, each time you reach out a helping hand, you're helping (an aspect of) yourself.

There are never any mistakes in those we meet daily. I attract those who can serve me and those I can serve. Some of the meetings may seem trivial as we pass a friend at the grocery store and merely say a few words, but even that exchange has profound and deep effects.

It never ceases to amaze me how smart God is. Being the Divine Intelligence Who "knows everything" as it simultaneously occurs is simply staggering to the human mind. Keeping it all in Divine Order, being on top of events as they occur, makes this unseen Power far more incredible

than human words can say. (God must be a mother, huh? Knows all . . . sees all . . . handles all. . . .)

While in Rhode Island, I spent the first day healing individuals. Following the appointments, I returned to the home of my hostess to have dinner and change so I could speak from 6:30 to 8:30 that evening.

Erin, a teenager, had flown in from Connecticut to Rhode Island and was having an acupuncturist work on her. I'd never witnessed this type of healing modality. Since I know myself so well, being a motormouth, coupled with curiosity of all the questions I knew I would have, I asked if I could watch him work on Erin. I certainly didn't want my speaking to interrupt what he needed to do. He immediately gave permission.

Actually, you would have been proud of me. My voice was a whisper and we discovered quickly that rather than speaking and being a pest, I was actually available to be used as a tool for Erin and the acupuncturist.

Gloria, why, at age thirteen, was Erin seeking this kind of help?

One day her brother was driving and as he found himself transferring from a bridge to the regular roadway, he felt his back wheels hydroplaning and preparing to pull the back end of the truck over the cliff. He thought quickly, believing if he punched the accelerator, it would bring the tires out of the magnetic pull that was surely going to become a disaster. However, as he did, the truck's rear end swung sharply around with full force into a tree.

Within the vehicle a television rested on a solid oak stand, which broke free from the impact and hit Erin in the head. She went into a coma immediately, and the doctors suggested that they pull the plug. They believed there was no hope.

God bless her little heart, as well as her parents. Oh my gosh, Gloria, so many of us don't even realize how fortunate we are not to have those tragedies in our lives. I certainly hope there's a happily-ever-after to this one, or I won't be able to stand it. Hearing such stories, concerning children, is almost more than I can bear.

After several months of being in an unconscious state, Erin regained consciousness. Her motor skills were sluggish, but what bothered her most was her left arm. When it remained straight, you would have never known Erin had suffered such a head trauma, except for the slow and careful way she spoke. However, if she bent her arm at the elbow, for any length of time, it began to quiver. If she didn't straighten her arm immediately, it would make her entire body shake . . . and at age thirteen, she wanted to die of embarrassment.

Erin's mother said she and her husband were fortunate that Erin was underage to make such choices, because several times Erin had almost convinced doctors to take her directly into brain surgery and cut those nerves that made her arm shake. Erin was willing to try anything.

Erin lay upon the massage table in the home where I was staying while in Rhode Island. There are no coincidences. Loving kids the way I do, it was completely natural for me to hold her fingers, tickle her arm, and take the privilege of sensing her body as the acupuncturist did what he knew how to do. Very quickly, I became aware that whenever he put a needle into Erin, I could feel the sensation in my body. Erin doesn't hurt anywhere because of the accident. Instead, she is numb, which doesn't help doctors (or acupuncturists) know, except through book knowledge, what to do.

This is all so fascinating to me. I'm wondering, as you speak, if many of the pains I've felt in my life "were mine" or "someone else's that I was carrying." I'm going to pay very close attention to your teachings so I can have clarity and understanding on this issue.

Erin's body became my body. I could feel where the nerves were pinched in the left upper arm, in the elbow, running down into the wrist. I could feel the weakness and could barely lift my arm. The block of energy and damage in the left upper arm almost brought tears to my eyes, as if it was blood raw. (Thank goodness Erin couldn't feel it, or it would have been excruciating.)

I told the acupuncturist my sensations. As I told and pointed to the spots of discomfort, he knew immediately where to place the needles. Within moments of having the needles inserted, I could feel relief in various areas. Working on Erin became a game for the doctor and for me. He, for the first time on an extremely subtle level, was receiving validation for the work he does. It served us well. Until that moment, I had never thought of working beside doctors, in hospitals, maybe in the nursery units to tell doctors where babies were hurting since they are unable to do so, themselves.

That evening, while working on Erin, my attention was drawn to a clock on the bookcase. It was 6:20 P.M. I had to be at the church at 6:30 for my Friday night talk. Yikes and I hadn't even put on my dress or brushed my teeth. Lucky for me, the church was only minutes away from where I was staying. I'm sure the audience wouldn't have cared if we'd had to begin late, had they known what I'd been delayed for.

The following day, Erin and her mother attended my workshop and stayed until they had to catch their flight back to Connecticut. Erin saw the Light. Earlier that morning, I'd laid hands on her and felt how "slow" the inner movements of her mind had become. I was pleased to feel all the reconnections beneath my hands. I excitedly shared with her that, as difficult as her past learning was and how much extra added effort it took just to understand those things she was being taught, they would now once again come easily. Erin glowed that afternoon, and I'm sure she will put all she learned that weekend into practice.

God is the Source of Divine Love, and thanks for reminding me to be an outlet for that love.

As the loving energy flows from the Source to others, we, the conduits, can't help but enjoy the luxuries "of being used." I've always believed that a miracle is anything born of love, which can be even something as simple as sweeping a floor or folding a load of laundry.

By the way, I even thought that if people didn't like my style of writing or my personality, I'd just change careers and become a Rainbow vacuum cleaner salesman. (God, I love that vacuum. And besides, *cleanliness is next to Godliness.*)

12

I Work for God, and
Money Works for Me

A woman, in financial trouble, called me last week and asked how to get out of a possible forthcoming bankruptcy. She was also angry that her metaphysical beliefs weren't working for her.

I asked if she had creditors calling and she replied, "Yes." I asked how she was dealing with them and she said, "I'm ignoring their calls."

Well, by golly, the Universe was ignoring her and her husband's calls, as well. I'm not sure why people think the adage, "What goes around, comes around" refers to them *only when they do acts of kindness.* In truth, the more you give, the more you have to give. Isn't it amazing? People who are not conscious of this . . . who still attempt to sneak freely into my workshops, leave empty donation envelopes for healings—get the adage all wrong. Or just *don't* get it.

In the above situation, I insisted that she stop resisting immediately. I urged her to feel embarrassed and completely express it, in writing, to each debtor. She is One with the debtor. I asked her to realize, "I am in harmony with my debts and debtors."

"If you are withholding someone's good/love—the invisible world will withhold yours." I encouraged her to offer to repay all debts, because the electric company had given her the electricity, trusting she would pay. Issuers of credit cards also trusted her or they wouldn't have allowed her to buy merchandise now and to pay later. What an honor it is to be trusted! We must prove ourselves trustworthy by fulfilling our obligations. Responsibility and accountability are important, especially to someone who is spiritually aware.

I believe the biggest error humans make is believing "it is our job to make a living." If God is our very life and being, we should also understand that "it's His business" to take care of us. It's not my home. I live in the house of God. My businesses (Miracle Healing Ministry and Miracle Publishing Company) are God's businesses. It's not my clothing . . . it's God appearing as clothing. My mind is an individual tool for spiritual good to express through. Our bodies, though individual in appearance are "many," in spiritual reality they are "One Body," the Body of Christ/Light. I have freely offered my mind, body, and soul to Spirit to be used for the greater good of humanity.

Gloria, I just want you to know that I don't plan on interrupting you or asking questions while you're discussing this. I need to be a very good listener and not try to pre-plan what I will ask. I need to be in the moment and hear everything you have to say concerning this teaching.

As we reunite, through awareness that God is the debtor, we will also have the manifestation of the money needed, as God appearing as the supply necessary.

If we find ourselves overextended, like this woman, a promise of attempting to pay (even a compliment or gratitude) can make all the difference in the world. Being willing, rather than resisting, will remove the blocks that prevent us from experiencing the greater good.

Think of the person you owe as yourself. This simple realization opens your heart. Choosing to give allows the infinite flow to appear. As you choose to give, the abundance, which is already established within you, becomes an avenue of expression in the physical.

People judge money every day, in every way. Those who have a poverty consciousness judge it as good when they have money, and bad when they don't. Rather than admiring the accomplishments of those who have financial success, they hate them. The poor are judged because they're on welfare, and the rich are judged if they don't give money.

The romantic version of Robin Hood is misleading, taking from the rich and giving it to the poor. When you awaken to the infinite, spiritual state of consciousness, you don't have to take . . . you accept and allow. See how often you can graciously accept even a compliment. If it's difficult to accept a gift, in that form, perhaps you'll understand that no one, except yourself, is withholding your greater good on a financial level. (Practice saying thank you to every compliment and you'll see a natural supplying flow in your finances, as well.)

Recently, a woman called and asked me, "Why do we want to give up the judgment of those things that appear as good?" I used winning the grand-prize lottery as an example. In a person's mind, it's good if they win (and have money) and bad to be without it. Which, by the way, is what keeps people from experiencing financial freedom . . . the *belief* in dual powers, good *and* bad, disease *and* health, rich *and* poor.

If you truly believe in God and know God is good, then God *is health, prosperity, and All That Is Good.* If you believe in this good, your experience is good. If you believe in good and bad, you experience both, for you have been given free will.

If you win the money, you would judge the situation as good because you would believe you now have financial security. (You're still attempting to make yourself a better humanhood, rather than living spiritually with One Power.) However, once you have the money, under karmic law, it comes with lessons and experiences.

One of which may be that you don't know if your friends like you because of you or because of your money. Users may come out of the woodwork, requesting it. You now have to judge "who deserves it" and "who doesn't." You may, through human opinion and what you think is based upon good judgment, lend (or give) the money to someone who misuses it, along with your friendship. You've now experienced a lesson, usually painful and humanly disappointing. Every time you judge a person, place, or thing, it's an immediate reminder to return to Oneness.

A woman invited me to lunch one day. When the check arrived, I offered to pay for the meal. She said, "Oh, no, let me get it. After you become rich and famous, I know you'll take care of me." **WRONG.** My human emotions of anger and disappointment, coupled with disgust, made me not want to be around this person any longer. My judgment of the situation had to be healed later. We all meet daily judgments in countless forms. Here's the bright side: each of us will get plenty of practice, reminding us of Oneness.

You believe winning the lottery would be good because you could put the money to good use. How do you, as a human, even attempt to believe that you can see the "whole plan" and know what's good or bad for yourself or another person?

A man, observing a butterfly emerge from its cocoon, watched it struggle. (By the way, this is a true story.) He cut the branch from the tree and took it into his home where he cut away the cocoon. Shortly after the butterfly emerged, it died. He went to his local library and researched this process, only to find that it is through the struggle to emerge from the cocoon that a butterfly's body becomes smaller and the wings stronger. Through his human intervention, he had weakened the creature, rather than allowing it to struggle and attain the necessary strength to survive.

Daily, as humans, we do the same thing with our loved ones. Giving/lending money when our heart says we shouldn't. Or when we offer out of obligation, rather than love. Money is one of the best tools to teach us how to listen to our hearts. Since we don't humanly see the whole picture, we must turn within, receive our guidance, and act accordingly.

As a healer, I was told "no" only once, in the beginning years, not to help another to achieve freedom from disease. I was told, by Spirit, to back off because the woman needed to heal it herself, which would give her the confidence to help others. She did heal herself and helped hundreds of others *because I listened to my heart and said, "No."* What I humanly thought, or misunderstood as selfish of me, actually empowered her.

Years ago, I met a man who charged $400 per hour for his services. Business was failing and he came to me for help. I gave him an hour of my time and he received peace and understanding. As we finished, I asked, "What was my time worth to you?" Shocked, because he knew I didn't charge, he sputtered quickly, "A hug." I looked him in the eye and replied, "Hugs don't put food on my table."

Frightened (and embarrassed, I'm sure), he stated almost in question form, "Well, maybe ten dollars?"

"You believe your time is worth four hundred dollars per

hour, but consider that my talents and gifts are worth only ten dollars per hour." At that point, I asked him for a ten dollar bill, which was bold of me to do.

When he placed the money in my hands, I replied, "You might charge an extraordinary sum of money for your business dealings, but in reality, *because I am One with you,* your underlying belief is that it's really only worth ten dollars."

With that teaching, I wrote these words on his ten dollar bill. "There's plenty for everyone. Give freely and with love." I handed it back to him. As I placed the money in his hand, I explained that he had given the gift to me and I was *gifting* it back to him. I suggested he take the money into the next store and buy something of beauty with it, allowing the blessing to continue for both of us.

The Bible says, "It's harder to get a rich man into heaven than it is to get a camel into the eye of a needle." I asked Spirit one day what that meant. In my quiet time, I was guided with this understanding. In olden days, the eye of a needle was a "garage" where they parked camels during the night. It was a small dwelling, with an igloo cutout opening as the door. The shepherds would have to force the camel to kneel and crawl through the opening. Once inside, the camels would arise and were penned in. It was both difficult and frustrating.

Getting those who are fearful concerning money to open their minds to the heavenly state of consciousness is difficult because they are attempting to acquire, hoard, and be selfish concerning what they assume is important. They fear they can't experience wealth and be spiritual at the same time. Many in this dimension believe that money talks and those who have the most are the ones with the most power.

One of Nikki's friends invited us to lunch one afternoon.

Bob asked, "Gloria, you're not afraid of me, are you?" I was taken completely by surprise, not expecting such a question. I was honest: the thought had never entered my mind that I was supposed to be afraid of him.

"That's just it. I'm a large man and most people are frightened of me, and I'm definitely respected. When I speak, people listen."

I was still in confusion that I was supposed to be frightened of him and told him so.

He said, "Well, you scare the hell out of me."

I laughed and referred to my size, soft voice, and nonthreatening nature and he said, "But, you are so-o-o powerful."

I laughed. I guess if Love is all power, then to a large degree, I am growing to "all-powerful."

A man, attempting to share his beliefs with me on the teachings of two powers, added, "I'm not trying to change your beliefs, Gloria." I interrupted before he could say, "But," as I replied, "Good. Because **you** don't have the power to do that. In fact, no one does."

When I speak of abundance, it doesn't appear in just dollars. Also, please don't open yourself to the Presence, thinking *If I just do this God-thing, I'll have all the money I need*, because you will be very disappointed. You can't "use" God or try to bring Him into the human scene. If you will open yourself to the Presence, He will take you to a state of consciousness where all "things appear, usually before you know you need them."

Who has the most power, investments, toys, and treasures surrounding them? That doesn't measure the richest person in the world, spiritually speaking. Spiritual wealth comes in the form of a daily sense of peace that, as you need something, it appears, whether it comes in the form of continued health, clothing, relationships, vacations, food, or spiritual understanding. Worry about financial situations vanishes once you're aware that everything that you shall ever need already exists and you open yourself to your Oneness with it. Not will be, can be, but already is and *allowing* the Divine Intelligence to manifest it before you.

I don't worry much about money. I ordered a "Peek-a-Bow Gift-Wrap Sack" from my friend Robyn to give to my mother for her birthday. Robyn charged me $40, which I gladly paid. I also asked her to make one for me. Since I'm so organized, the bag would serve me well to keep the gift wrap, bows, tape, and scissors in one tidy bag. However, when I ordered the bag for myself, I didn't actually have the $40. Robyn had agreed to deliver the bag to me on Tuesday, three days away.

On Tuesday, people who had flown from Virginia to Montana with their baby, for a private healing, had arrived. The child didn't really need me. His energy was only a tiny bit imbalanced around his heart, which would have corrected itself without my help. When I finished, they asked, "What do we owe you?"

"Nothing. Don't be silly. You spent so much money on airfare, lodging, and the concern of your child. You owe me nothing."

I walked the people to their car and said our good-byes. I returned to the house and in the kitchen, lying on the table, were two twenty-dollar bills. Minutes later, Robyn arrived with my gift bag and I was able to transfer the funds into her hands. I didn't need the money because it was the bag itself I wanted. The money would appear to be revenue of a go-between, but it never actually had a moment to touch my hands.

Only humanly do we think that we need the money first. If we look to our Oneness with it (the desire), and the realization that it already is within us, and give thanks that IT

IS ALREADY TAKEN CARE OF, we can bypass the currency. The most common error most people make (myself included) in their prayers or metaphysical attempts to manifest their desires is asking (or visualizing) and then doubting. We also humanly wonder "when and how it can ever occur." Please remember. I am speaking from experience.

When I think, "I need something," now that I'm continuing to grow and spiritually understand that while I'm teaching others, I do the following:

- I realize my Oneness with God, Who constitutes my Oneness with all spiritual being, ideas, and creations.
- I realize that what I seek is already established with me. (Within the consciousness of God, Who created me. It's already made manifest in the spiritual kingdom/Divine consciousness.) **I give my thanks, for affirming it's already accomplished allows the manifestation in physical reality.**
- If I find myself trying to humanly figure it out (or force it to occur), I realize almost immediately that I am creating a separation from my greater good. Spirit doesn't withhold my goodness; human fear and doubt do. Therefore, I recognize my fear and doubt, resisting not, nor pretending I'm not feeling or thinking it. I realign myself in harmony with the fear and doubt, and I watch miracles made manifest. (Also, I don't "think" it already exists, "I KNOW" it does.)

When Jesus was feeding the multitudes, He didn't ask the Heavenly Father for the cash so He could go purchase the food. He gave His blessings and thanks for the food, *knowing it already existed* and through direct manifestation, He was capable of feeding the people.

When you no longer love, hate, or fear money, you will have dissolved all human judgments concerning it. Money just *is* God appearing in form. I have witnessed the abundance, within spiritual consciousness, and without a doubt—there *is* plenty for everyone. With authority I have spoken, but the greater understanding must come to you personally, not in the form of words, but through experience.

When we surrender our human judgments about money, realizing our Oneness with it, we rise above karmic law, which manifests as today, plenty; tomorrow, lack. Once we arrive at the state of consciousness where there is only One Power and no further human "opinions" concerning it, there is only One experience—prosperity. Which, of course, is always (spiritually) good because it has no dual opposite.

Try this exercise the next time your mind starts to race with judgments concerning money or anything else. A reminder: Whatever fears or concern fills your mind, silently state, *I have no opinion concerning this.* If the human mind can't yak about how good something is or how terribly bad, it silences. In silence is peace, and in peace is God and His all-good, ever awaiting you to be self-realized.

Never seek for abundance in any physical form, because the desire for it will hold you under karmic law, experiencing dual powers. Realize that which you seek is already established "within you" and release it. Surrender the desire by closing your eyes, opening your mind to the violet Light/Presence of God, and all else will be added.

I was shown a vision of stacks and stacks of money, banded like they are in banks. The money was piled approximately five stories high, five miles wide, and went from my visible view to infinity. That was the inner Fort Knox. I'm not to look to the outer and seek it, but knowing that abundance is already within my state of consciousness,

I allow it to flow into the outer world of form. I then find, personally, that I write books, songs, perform healings, create games or toys, and other forms to open the channels for supply to appear.

When I have performed healings, following the heart-to-heart hug, people have opened their wallets to hand me money. I ask them to place their donation in a privately sealed envelope and give the gift to my assistant. I don't hold judgments toward money, but I never want "one to influence the other." I am going to give, without measure, without ever thinking of what I might get out of it in return.

My abundance appears from giving, not receiving. Most people believe wealth is from what they acquire, but in spiritual reality, your abundance is in how much you have to give, not how much you receive.

If you aren't experiencing affluence on all levels, think of giving to start the flow. If you are already a giving person, then perhaps you need to "give up" something; usually it's fear. (Which is dissolved as you open yourself to the Presence.) It may be envy that you "give up" that others seem to have "it" and you don't. Be in harmony with those feelings and your fears.

I'm just sharing what works for me. You see, I work for God and money always works for me.

13

Anyone Can Stay
at the Waldorf

Excuse me, ol' buddy, ol' pal—I just became aware that I was starting to sound "better than others," as if I never get scared or stressed out. And that's just not true. Forgive me if I was starting to sound superior.

Gloria, you didn't sound cocky to me. What I heard through your teachings was a tone of authority and confidence. Those of us who are attempting to make a better life for ourselves would want our leader to be strong and confident.

That word, "confident," reminds me of a business trip I took to New York City. The businessman I was flying in to see reserved a room for me at the Waldorf Astoria. I live in a conservative tract home and cut coupons to stretch my grocery dollars. When I arrived at the Waldorf, I felt intimidated by the women who wore designer clothes and diamonds. I was in awe of the surroundings and the new sights and sounds. (We don't even have a taxi or a stoplight in our town.)

At lunch, this man expressed his disappointment that he

hadn't had time to show me around New York City and promised that during my next visit, he would make arrangements for me to stay at the Plaza and entertain me at the Four Seasons. Humbly, I said, "If it's much grander than all this, I don't know if I could stand it."

He replied, "Gloria, I never bought that hillbilly act of yours for a single second. The first time you walked into my conference room, to meet with my people and me, you entered with an air of sophistication and confidence I've never seen before.

"Sir," I responded, "I don't know if I'm sophisticated . . . or a hillbilly . . . maybe I'm just a chameleon and can blend in well no matter where you put me."

I love seeing life through your eyes. For just a fleeting moment, it was as if I was watching a movie inside my head. I felt like I'd been part of your experience.

I am sophisticated. I am a hillbilly. I am One with all that is. Being both means that I'll meet you where you are. If you need me to be sophisticated, I'll "try 'n act like a lady." If you need me to hang out at a bar-be-que picnic and smoke 'n drink 'n cuss, I can do that, also. Those are all aspects of who I am.

I am a reflection of you. I have your strengths, your weaknesses, and am overcoming the same fears. Like you, I'm a good person and a great spirit. I can also be a real butthead at times. I'm just me, doing the best I can with the awareness I have.

I accept you for who you are, I accept you for all you're not, and I accept you for all you can be. I also accept that everyone won't like me, the way I speak publicly, or my style of writing. I don't take it personally and I'll explain that more in depth, later, during our time together.

We're in Spokane. I've never been here before . . . what a beautiful city. The two mountain passes we crossed to get here were just gorgeous, but the city itself is so green and alive with energy as well.

I love Spokane, too, and always thought if I left Montana, I'd want to have a home in this city. It's where my public career began on October 5, 1995. I have received so much support from the people in this area; they are my extended family.

Tonight, I'll be speaking at the Metaphysical Research Society, where I began my journey so long ago. It's going to be a reunion for me to see my friends once again.

During my first weekend in Spokane, I brought my daughter Jaime with me to handle book sales. Before we left home, I received a letter from an older couple, inviting us to stay at their home then—or whenever I was in the area. They appreciated the charitable work I provided to people without gouging or focusing on the almighty dollar. In the letter, they apologized "that they lived simply," but offered their hearts and home to my daughter and me.

As Jaime and I were driving toward Spokane, she asked, "But, Mom, what if *simply* means they don't have indoor plumbing? We will get a motel then, right?"

"No, Jaime. If they live simply, and we have to use an outhouse, we'll be gracious guests." That made her very nervous.

When we arrived at Fred and Dorothy's, "simple" would have made your head swim. They live in a beautiful house on top of a hill, overlooking Spokane. Their house is filled with furniture that Fred has made, they served delicious food they had organically grown, and they were giving beyond words.

For the two years I did healings in Spokane every other weekend Fred and Dorothy's home became my home-away-from home. Their house had an upper level apartment with two bedrooms, a kitchen, bath, and living room where I could go after a long day of miracle working.

Fred and Dorothy are like parents to me, loving, wise, and living the spiritual life by example. At the end of a long day, I'd return, "Oh honey, I'm home." Early morning spiritual discussions with Dorothy filled me with love to meet each day. Like caring parents, these people would ask me to awaken them, if I returned late, to know I had arrived home safely.

They're now in their eighties, but I'll never forget what Dorothy said when we first met. "Gloria, you're in your forties and you can do all this. You're going to continue to evolve, and Fred and I are going to stick around to see what you're able to do when you're our age."

Gloria, will these people mind that you're bringing an extra guest?

They won't mind at all. I used to travel with one or two companions and each of us was wholeheartedly accepted. Once, during a working weekend, I brought two copilots, Nikki and June. Nikki and I shared a room and gave June her private space. During the night, I was awakened with a moaning voice, "Gloria, help . . ." From a sound sleep, I awoke startled and sat up in bed.

"Nikki. Wake up—Dorothy needs me!" She and I ran through the upper apartment, down the stairs in the dark, and through the door that leads to the rest of the house. Approaching Dorothy's bedroom, I was asking, "Dorothy? What's wrong? Do you need help?" Dorothy was sleeping.

I apologized to Nikki; I had awakened her for nothing. I

wasn't even sure how I could have heard Dorothy from the bottom floor, but I could have sworn I'd heard a cry for help.

We returned to bed. Nikki immediately fell back to sleep, but I was pondering if I had dreamed the urgent cry for help.

In a moaning tone, a second time, "Gloria, help. . . ." THERE. I HEARD IT AGAIN.

"Nikki. Wake up—I heard it again."

"Maybe it's Fred," I nearly shouted.

For a second time, we began the run through the house. On my way past the bathroom, I noticed a night-light that silhouetted my friend June. I opened the door and asked if she had been calling out to me. She had. She was very ill. I did a healing and everyone was able to return to bed.

I'm sure that Fred and Dorothy felt secure when you were around, as do your friends and family. I know I would.

I feel secure knowing Fred and Dorothy are there for me, as well. I think the reason we have such a wonderful relationship is because it's based on unconditional love. Neither they, nor I, are asking anything from one another. Our friendship, for one another, is the gift itself. No expectations or demands are asked. They were right. They do live simply. They just simply love.

Also, please don't look to me as if you'll never be able to accomplish these same things. It will take practice, and I'll give you another example concerning that. But for now, we're here at Fred and Dorothy's.

I'll help you get your luggage to your room and get you settled in. Take some time to freshen up for my speaking engagement tonight, and then I'll introduce you to my "adopted parents." You're going to absolutely love the bed, pillows, and homemade quilts and comforters. I'll be lucky if I can even get you out of bed in the morning. But if I can, you're going to feel like a million dollars. I've never spent a night in this house without feeling refreshed and fully energized to begin the new day.

If you don't mind, we'll have a late dinner, after my twenty-minute speech. I don't like to speak publicly on a full tummy. Maybe we could just have a little yogurt or fruit to tide us over.

Your room looks out over all of Spokane, and tonight when it's dark, you'll see all the beautiful lights below and the stars within reach.

Gloria, I can already feel the love in this house and I feel so honored to meet these loved ones of yours. In my opinion, anyone could stay at the Waldorf, but it's very special to stay at Fred and Dorothy's.

14

Lighten Up!
(Friday Night Speech)

Good evening, ladies and gentlemen. It's so wonderful to be back in Spokane. If you remember, I never preplan what I'm going to say in a speech. I never know what's going to fall out of my mouth or the direction the teachings will take. I can only listen to my thoughts and be guided by Spirit. As a speaker, I don't know what is important for each of you to hear, but I do know this . . . those of you, here tonight, are not here by chance.

I've met countless people over the years who hear me speak or read my books and respond, "But, Gloria, I don't experience miracles every day of my life and I don't see a Master Teacher manifest." They also relate that they're not sure whether they've ever felt the Presence of God, or whether they'd even recognize it. Tonight, ladies and gentlemen, I'm going to guarantee that every single one of you will feel the Presence of God and each will experience a miracle.

In order to do that, though, I'd like to ask you to stand and do things only as I ask you to. Pick a partner next to you. Does everyone now have a partner? Good. We can begin.

I'd like you to rub your hands together and pull them apart, approximately an inch away from each other. Do you feel the warmth? Some tingling? That's energy. You can't see it, but you can feel it.

Now, rub your hands together again and face them toward your partner's hands, approximately an inch apart. Do you still feel tingling? Can you feel any warmth coming from your partner's hands? Again, you can't "see," it—but you can feel it.

Now, rub your hands together and place your fingertips together, pointing toward the ceiling . . . your hands should resemble a tepee shape above your partner's head. This is the crown chakra area. Can you sense warmth or energy from the top of your partner's head?

And now, drop your arms around each other, for a great big hug—because you're feeling the Presence of God and you're the greatest miracle of all.

Oh—and while you're standing, you may as well clap . . . I always tell Kirk, after I've been out speaking and teaching, "I got another standing ovation." (He doesn't know I make you guys do this. . . .)

Well, alrighty then, let's all just take a nice, long, deep breath . . . and exhale. Let the fun begin.

A friend of mine was having a grand opening for her business. To support her, I agreed to teach "The Master's Program," and she had asked me to walk among her customers that evening, introducing the class and myself. I was a social butterfly that evening, going from one to the next, offering "magic kisses and healing hugs." I was so filled with the spirit of joy that evening, it was like I was walking on clouds.

I remember one man in particular. As I hugged him, he replied, "My back doesn't hurt while you're holding me, Gloria." At the time this occurred, I wasn't aware of the healing energy that flowed through me.

We released from the hug and he said, "My back hurts again—give me another hug." You see, the love that I felt that night for others, and the love I'd felt for others throughout my life was automatically renewing people's spirits before I was ever conscious of it. And so it is with you.

My friend had hired an enlightened speaker for that evening and she'd been told that he was a popular comedian as well. Chairs were placed on a patio and the crowd was comfortably seated. The speaker welcomed us and began speaking as if what he was saying was memorized. I, for one, couldn't feel anything genuine or true from the "words" he was sharing. He couldn't seem to capture the audience's attention, and I was beginning to feel sorry for him. He must have been so embarrassed.

Seeing that his "enlightenment and wisdom" wasn't working, he decided to allow the comedian in him to come out for entertainment. He asked the crowd if they had questions. No hands were raised. He offered to answer anyone's questions, whether they were from a spiritually based need or a random need concerning the physical dimension. Still no hands were raised.

I raised my hand and asked, "I'm trying to be so spiritual. Why do I still yell at my kids?" The crowd, as well as the speaker, was totally silent. You could have heard a pin drop. The speaker hesitated, as if he was thinking of an answer, then startled the crowd by yelling, one word at a time, into the microphone, "I . . . DON'T . . . KNOW—WHY . . . DO . . . YOU . . . YELL . . . AT . . . YOUR . . . KIDS?"

The crowd, including me, roared with laughter. It was

the only funny thing he'd had to say all night. In reply to his question, I said, "Probably because they drive me nuts at times. They should have been carpenters, because they just about hammer me to death."

My friend took the microphone away from the speaker, during the break, and put it into my hands. I wasn't "enlightened" at that time. I was just a housewife and mom, and I'm not sure I had any good advice that evening that I could give away. But, I do remember telling jokes. The audience definitely needed to "lighten up."

There isn't one of us in this room, tonight, who doesn't need to do the same. We find so many stresses in today's society—even the stress of attempting "to stay on the path," be more open to heal, or to spiritually understand and incorporate what we learn.

I'm feeling pretty silly tonight. Love tickles my tummy sometimes and I feel like a kid again. I once told my best friend, Nikki, "I can't help it, Nik. I feel as if I'm still eighteen years old and I can't help feeling childlike." Nikki remarked sharply, "Fourteen, honey. You act as if you're fourteen years old. . . ."

During a walk one evening with my daughter Jaime, around the neighborhood, a policeman stopped and rolled down his window. I thought, "Oops. I should have my dog, Roco, on a leash." I was surprised that he didn't care that the dog was walking loose at my side.

"How old are you?" he sharply asked. Thinking he was referring to my daughter, I responded, "Jaime? She's nearly twenty-two years old."

Harshly, he stated, "I'm not talking about her. I'm talking about you," as his index finger pointed sharply out his window toward me.

Surprised at this officer's attitude, and feeling as if this was going to embarrass him worse than he had been for a very long time, I raised my sunglasses and replied, "Sir, in another week, I'll be forty-six years old."

I was right. He was embarrassed and "tried to flatter me."

"I thought you were a teenager and I was going to ticket you for smoking under age."

You see, I didn't "manifest these wrinkles for nothing." My appearance alone *proves* God has a sense of humor or he wouldn't have given me "elf lips" and tiny features that make everyone think I look like an elf.

Maybe it's partly the bells on my shoes that have something to do with that. When my daughter Danielle and I were back-to-school shopping, I said, "Hey. Danielle. While we're downtown shopping, let's run down to the corner shop to see if they have any new L.A. Gear Light shoes in."

Rolling her eyes, she said, "Oh, God, Mom. I wish you would just grow up."

A woman standing nearby, also back-to-school shopping, overheard Danielle's remark and laughed. She giggled, "Isn't it funny? We're always saying that to our kids . . . who would have ever thought they could think that of us also?"

Realizing that I was an embarrassment to my child, I said, "Sorry, Danielle. I'll stop wearing bells immediately."

"Oh, no, Mom, you can't stop wearing bells. That's your trademark. But you could stop wearing those stupid shoes that blink when you walk." (I *like* those "stupid" shoes, and wish they weren't so few and far between in Montana.)

At any rate, childlike, or child*ish*, I'm feeling playful right now. So, how about if ol' Dr. Glo-bug lightens things up some more? Laughter, by the way *is* the best medicine and exercise. It raises your heart rate and it also exercises your stomach muscles. Laughter is aerobic. Gosh, we can lose weight by being happy.

A man is painting a church, but it's such a beautiful day, he wants to get out on the golf course. He's nearing the top of the church and is running low on paint. Rather than coming down off the ladder and refilling his supply, he adds paint thinner and continues. As he gets to the top of the steeple, he finds that once again—he's not going to have enough paint to finish the job without coming down off the church.

He looks at those beautiful blue skies and feels the warmth of the sun as his thoughts fantasize of making that hole-in-one today. As before, he adds more paint thinner and continues.

As he comes down off the ladder and his feet are planted squarely upon the earth once again, he notices that storm clouds have gathered. Lightning strikes, and a downpour of rain follows . . . washing all the paint away.

A booming voice says, "Repaint, repaint—and thin no more."

I love religious jokes. Here's another one:

A nun is in a football stadium, surrounded by three men who are mocking her religion. The first man says, "Hey. Why don't we move to Florida? I hear that not many Catholics live there." The second man says, "No way. Let's move to Alaska—I've heard that not many Catholics live there." The third man replies, "No, no . . . let's move to Arkansas—I've heard that not many Catholics live there."

The nun sweetly smiles and says, "Why don't you all just go to hell?" They looked shocked, of course, not expecting such a reply as she sweetly and lovingly says, "There are *no* Catholics there. . . ."

I had gotten a call from an eighty-five-year-old woman who had attended one of my workshops with her husband.

The elderly woman asked, "Gloria, would you close your eyes and tell me what I look like long distance?"

As I closed my eyes and "realized my Oneness with this woman," my inner vision opened and I said, "Mrs. Richardson, all I see is total violet Light. You are filled with pure, Divine energy and there wouldn't be anywhere else to put any, unless it was in your pocketbook." She giggled and said, "I'm going to put Louie on the phone—would you tell him what you just told me?"

As I repeated the experience to Mr. Richardson, he said, "Well, it's like this, Gloria. Last night, Mabeldine was hurting badly. I looked at your book and your face is on the front, and your face is on the back—and you wrote that book, so that book *is you*."

He continued, "So I laid the book on my solar plexus last night and it filled me up with violet Light, and then I just put my hand on Mabeldine's solar plexus and it filled her up, too."

I can't believe I said this: "Mr. Richardson, please don't tell people you're sleeping with me now."

We all had a good laugh with that and I've actually told the story countless times across the nation. Others in my workshops have shared similar stories, "I couldn't get an individual appointment with Gloria, but used her book as a tool—and got my miracle anyway."

The reason *Go Within or Go Without* or even the information you read in this book has the ability to heal is because of the state of consciousness from which it has been or is being written. (Oh, there goes that glowing warmth around my head again—I'm having a power surge as the energy fills me.) As a person is open to the Presence of God, sitting and listening or reading the words, they receive their miracles—not from any magic in me saying anything, because it's not the words that are healing. It is the consciousness, pouring *through* the words, that is the healing agent.

My friend's guest speaker didn't "make his connection" and his speech was "empty words." I share this only to help make you aware, in your everyday experience, and particularly when you're paying large sums of money to hear someone teach.

We take everything so seriously, don't we? And, as metaphysicians, we're told that everything we see, touch, taste, smell, and hear is an illusion. That word "illusion" cracks me up. On stage in California, I was "mocking" that word as I swept my hands from head to foot down my four-foot-eleven height.

"This is all an illusion, folks." (Pausing . . . as a joker, because it's "all in the timing," I continued), "Because I'm really tall, sleek, and sexy."

I think the word illusion is what gives the metaphysical realm such a bad name. Because we're all "on this level" of trying to get ahead, make a buck, reach a dream, and handle the negative situations that continue to occur in our worlds. And whenever some joker/airhead tries to convince us that it's all an illusion or "in Divine Order," we get even more turned off to the idea of spirituality and metaphysics. When asked to meditate, we become sarcastic and say, "Maybe you have time to lie around all day and do nothing, but I'm a little busy working for a living."

It all seems pretty damn real when you feel pain emotionally or physically. It seems very real when you feel depressed or go through grief when your loved ones die of diseases that have no cures or hope. It doesn't feel like an illusion when the creditors are calling or you know you don't have enough money for groceries.

Even those who have been "on the path" for countless

years and spout all the "illusion and Divine Order" words, call me for uplifting and enlightenment. It's because they are just words and facts they have read from books. Until that state of consciousness is realized, those truths will "not work" in daily reality.

When we begin practicing, "Seeking the Kingdom of Heaven—which is within" we will discover that all else will be added in our outer world of form.

The Bible says, "Seek ye first the Kingdom of Heaven and all else will be added." It then says, "The Kingdom of Heaven is within." In my book *Go Within or Go Without,* I have taught you how to go within. If you don't mind, I don't want to rehash that in tonight's speech.

However, when your awareness shifts back within yourself, you begin growing at an extraordinary rate. As your consciousness rises above the belief of "having to work hard to get ahead," the "dog-eat-dog world," or "struggling to survive," levels that, until now, had you seeking from the outer world, you find those "illusions" altering. Things begin to get easier and it feels refreshing.

You begin experiencing Divine Order, Divine Timing, and harmony in everyday matters. And every day does matter.

To close, I'd like to quote a tale I wrote so you have a modern-day parable to remind you that the Presence of God is within you. There are leaders and there are followers; you're a responsible follower by choosing a responsible leader.

ALL ABOARD THE LOVE EXPRESS

Once upon a time, there was a Kingdom of Heaven and it was surrounded by various myths of obstacles that each must overcome in order to be granted admission. Prophets, seers (visionaries), and teachings of old had woven confusion around the kingdom with contradictory trains of thought. A commemoration was occurring wherein heaven and earth were becoming as One, so deemed as "A New Age for Humanity/A Spiritual Awakening." Many were called to aid in the transition and at present, few had answered.

However, false guides began springing up everywhere and they wanted to jump on the gravy train. They were aware that they could lead no one, for the way was unknown by them. Nevertheless, the masses were desperate and these false guides would be well paid for their services of deceit. Those who were conned would soon find that they had once more journeyed without distance.

One track was labeled the Love Express, but few were willing to attempt this route. *Love of self and others was the ticket,* but most got sidetracked with guilt, blame, condemnation, and judgment. Most believed there was a Conductor and only prayed He was keeping score of how many times they had attempted to stay on the right track.

Heaven is a mind filled with peace. A "State of Consciousness," not a place, and it was no secret that the only sacrifice that must be made was to lose all power to hurt self or others through thought, word, or deed. What a high price one must pay! And what was so good about heaven anyway? Also, in the insane world in which we live, how is it even possible?

One needs only to remember the legend of old: "With a man, it is indeed impossible, but with God, all things are possible." We know to follow no man, to not look without, but to seek within. To have our minds healed and restored to sanity is the Kingdom of Heaven made manifest in our lives and world. Those who paid the price of giving up the false values of prejudice, superiority, and conflict would, indeed, receive their just reward.

To those who follow another man: ask yourself these questions:

- Does he charge exorbitant prices, giving you little in return?
- Does he live like a king, at your expense?
- Does he share spiritual experiences in order to impress or convince you he is superior to you?
- Does he require your approval, admiration, and devotion?
- Does he belittle you, disregarding your feelings and suggestions?
- Does he require you to follow his exact methods and teachings, for his "is the only way?"
- Does he speak empty words?

If you have answered yes to the above, it is time to find a new teacher, for you are being taken for a ride. The ending of a relationship and experience has taught you discernment. *To follow an example* of one whose actions mirror his teachings, lives by his words, and offers Divine Teachings shall be your new beginning. You've just received your calling. The Kingdom of Heaven is awaiting you: *All Aboard the Love Express* . . .

Thank you for this time. Good night, be safe, be happy. . . . I love you all with my whole, great big heart.

15

Starlight . . . Star Bright

Oh, Gloria, that was a wonderful speech. I had tears in my eyes from laughing, and other times I felt weepy when you quoted your tale. It reminded me how I had always fantasized, as a child, that everyone in the world was good and kind like you are. I want to believe that it really is possible to live in a world filled with love.

Thank you, I'm so glad you enjoyed it. I love my life, I love my career, I love people, and I have wished people would just listen to me so they could say the same.

I also loved the part of your speech where you talked about the bells on your shoes. You even wear bells on your high heels. I thought it was cute that Danielle calls it your trademark.

I've worn bells on my shoes ever since I learned, through the angel Clarence of the classic movie *It's a Wonderful Life,* that every time a bells rings, an angel gets his wings. Years ago, I also had a little golden angel clipped to my shoelace in honor of Clarence. My sister Sheila said one day, "Gosh,

Gloria, your shoes light up when you walk, you have bells and an angel, do you have a horn . . . for when you're backing up?" In a very serious tone, I replied, "Now, wouldn't that be a little childish?"

I have countless cute stories concerning the effects of wearing bells, but my all-time favorite one occurred when a nine-year-old girl approached me one day. "I know why you wear bells on your shoes."

I thought, "How cute. She must have opened my book at random and read that part." When I stated that thought aloud, she said, "Oh, no, I read the whole book—in fact, I did a book report on it and got an 'A.' " I called her mother and asked if she'd fax me a copy of it *because I'd never been reviewed by a nine-year-old before.*

Across the fax, in a child's printing, the book report read:

A BOOK REPORT

BY: MARA PETERSON

Book: *Go Within or Go Without*
Author: Gloria Benish

The book is about Gloria and her healing powers. Her powers can heal heartache, headache, rheumatism, even AIDS. Once she even helped heal a man who had pain in his lungs. There's a saying that says, "Every time a bell rings, an angel gets his wings." Well, when Gloria heard that, she thought, "Hmmm . . . we need as many angels as we can get." So, she put bells on her shoes and went to do some errands; the bells were ringing everywhere.

I learned a lot from this book. I think it should become a classic.

I don't know about you, but I think Mara deserved an 'A.' The only part she didn't get right was, "it's not Gloria's powers." I'm just the instrument.

That is so sweet, Gloria. Children have so much to teach us. In order to enter heaven, we must become as little children. You're so tiny, and childlike, that's probably part of the reason you're capable of trusting and just purely loving life.

It's just my nature. It's just me. And, don't think I haven't been judged concerning my silliness, too.

Oh my gosh, look. There's the very first star for tonight. Although I'm not that far from the big 5 - 0 birthday, I always remember the "Starlight Star Bright" poem from when I was a child. I admit, I'd say it silently so I wouldn't get weird looks from people, but I rewrote it to fit myself. Now, whenever I see the first star of the night, I repeat this:

Starlight . . . Star Bright

Starlight . . . Star Bright . . .
I know I'm here to serve the Light.
I meditate, contemplate, and wait some more . . .
To have the stone rolled back from the invisible door.

Which leads to the wisdom of eyes unseen,
To review the scrolls from the King of Kings.
I know, within, that the game's being played,
But, the groundwork and rules haven't been easily laid.

I've processed my pain and forgiven my foe,
I've helped to spread love wherever I go.
What else must I do, to have this veil raised?
I feel powerless and ignorant, in fact, simply amazed.

For, in questioning Your timing, the answer arose,
Like a Phoenix from ashes, my reply is disclosed.
The mountain of impatience has returned to dust,
For all I've ever lacked, is to fully trust.

In Your Intelligence, Your Timing, and yes, Your Love, too.
In this moment, I feel like I've been born anew.
I'll take the backseat and leave the driving to You,
I won't ever again tell You what You should do.

I'll go where You take me, and speak if I must,
Now that I've learned to unwaveringly trust.

We're taught, as little children, to wish upon a star
and to believe without doubt that our wish will be
granted. Whether this is fact or fiction, the answer
will only be revealed to one who believes . . .

Starlight . . . Star Bright

Make a wish. It's real.

My wish already came true, Gloria. And I don't think I have to tell you what it is, do I?

I'm so glad you let me choose where to have dinner tonight. The Spaghetti Factory is my all-time favorite place to go, but I don't get to go very often since I have to drive four hours to do so. I always held my birthday celebrations at this restaurant because I had (and still have) so many low-income-based friends and it's affordable for a family night out. Yummers.

Well, my friend, this has been a very long day for you and I've given you so many things to think about. I'll just make sure you have everything you need and we can call it a night. I'm going to run down the steps to say goodnight to Fred and Dorothy, to see if they need anything also. I'll probably chat with them a few minutes too.

Three times, daily, I open myself to the Presence of God and do long distance healings for those on my prayer list. At 10:00 each night, I also "burn off any negativity" I've knowingly (or unconsciously) taken on during the day. This teaching is one of the "bits and pieces I'm aware of," that will be part of the twenty-minute speech I will give tomorrow night, so don't fear that I'll forget to tell you.

Give me a hug, my precious, good night . . . sleep tight, and don't let those derned ol' bed bugs bite . . .

16

Practice the Presence

Good morning, Dr. Glo-bug. Oh my gosh, you were so right about that bed. I barely slept at all; I was so pumped with energy after yesterday. But from the little sleep I did get, I do feel so refreshed and looking forward to another day with you.

It's so funny that you say, "how pumped with energy you were," because I used to wear my friend Nikki's hiney out. After a day of healing, I'd be flyin' the friendly skies because the energy that flows through me, to others, doesn't deplete me—it fills me to overflowing. I become "an energizer bunny." After a day of miracle working, I'd say, "Nikki. Let's go play." She said, "No. Let's go to bed . . ." I'm glad you had a good rest though.

You take care of your family's needs, and stand ready to assist strangers all day over the phone, in doing healings, or teaching workshops across the nation, as well as through-out the night. Don't you ever get tired?

Yes, I do. Before I ever caught a plane to go teach some-where, I cleaned the house, did laundry, prepared all the food for while I'd be gone, and made sure that a little part of me was in everything for my family. Kirk works a full-time job, and in making your life easier, I didn't want to make his harder.

In my mind, if I did all that, then I wasn't denying my family anything. At their meals, I was right there with them. But doing "my job" at home before I went to do "my job" for my career almost brought me to my knees.

I'll use a couple years ago as the example. I was taking courses to graduate with my Ph.D. (in religious studies), and I needed to teach 360 hours to qualify for my teaching credentials. Each workshop I teach is ten hours. That year, "because I couldn't say no," taking every opportunity to speak while people were willing to listen, I taught forty-six workshops across the nation. Four hundred and sixty hours, plus my "Stepford chores" and keeping track of accounting on books and maintaining two businesses. I was tired. I was tired beyond tired. Sizzled and frying.

No doubt, Gloria. You almost make me tired just listening to your full life.

I was thinking of "quitting." I was that exhausted. And then I met a woman, Barbara Vital, and my life was changed.

Have you read *Illusions* by Richard Bach? It's my all-time favorite book . . . one that Spirit allowed me to read in my beginning years. If you haven't read it, I highly recommend that you do. Richard wrote of the Reluctant Messiah, who could perform "tricks" that Christ did, and many we haven't heard about through the Bible. Although it's written as fiction, we, who have "ears to hear," know otherwise.

The messiah in the book becomes tired of people coming to him, to feed them, to inspire them, and mostly was tired of having to do the tricks in the first place to convince them.

I was feeling pretty darn sorry for myself, wondering why I had "chosen" to bite off so much and didn't have employees to help. Excuse me for whining, but I feel it's important for you to know all sides of me and the role I play for God. If you know that this same doubt and despair can come even after you "have a conscious realization of Oneness with God," then you won't pack your bags and take yourself on a guilt trip when it happens to you. I'm not sharing my busy life with you to make you feel guilty for reaching out for help. I'm telling you these things because you feel overwhelmed at times also, explaining that on each level it's a part of the growing experience.

I'm glad you're sharing these feelings, Gloria. Every time I hear you say something like that, it gives me hope that I'm okay the way I am. Here you do all these beautiful random acts of kindness for others and experience profound miracles, and you can be a little whiner-butt; still, and it doesn't "block" the progress of spiritually growing. You just have no idea how refreshing it is to hear that our negative emotions aren't keeping us from spiritual enlightenment and experiencing God in our lives. Thank you, thank you, thank you.

You're welcome. Your negative emotions are also an important and valid part of this experience. It's when we deny them or pretend we don't have them that gets us into trouble. I'll tell you more about that, too, but right now . . . I'm on a roll looking back into those days of "whine and roses" (as Kirk teases me about when I'm being a pill).

Back to Barbara. She was transplanted from Pennsylvania to the Bitterroot Valley. When she arrived in Montana, she found my book and found peace for the first time in her life. Being aware that I wear bells on my shoes and knowing, from the book, that I take nightly walks around the neighborhood, she began doing the same. She believed "we'd just run into each other casually and we could meet." She also began going to the local grocery store, "stopping, looking, and listening for the bells." She returned to the bookstore to pick up a book she'd ordered and when she told the owner what she was doing, in attempts to meet me, the owner said, "Why don't you just call her? Her phone number is in her book as well as in the telephone book." Barbara couldn't believe anyone would put her home telephone number in a book and the owner replied, "Gloria did."

Barbara and I connected and she brought a deaf lady to me. Within twenty minutes of leaving my home, the woman could hear again. Barbara then made an appointment for herself and had a personal revelation as my hands were upon her. She saw Christ kneeling at her side and during the experience she gasped and replied, "Oh my God, you've *always* been there, haven't you?" He smiled and nodded His head, "Yes."

Oh, heavy sigh, Glo-bug. I desire to know the Christ within me, my Higher Power. I'm so afraid I'm not doing things "right," or that I have the power to screw things up.

Be patient. Remember, always, we as humans can't manipulate this experience, but we can easily open ourselves to that Presence without the human force, and stand ready, with awareness, to receive It. And, you won't screw it up—I promise. You DON'T have the power to do so.

Following the healing, Barbara and I began a friendship. She told me about her dying son. He had received a blood transfusion, long before the general public knew about AIDS. Unaware, he met and married his true love and they had a child. The baby became quite ill and tests were taken, giving no indication of what was wrong. Her son Danny was extremely concerned, of course, and threatened the hospital that he would give them three more days to find out what was wrong with his child and if that challenge wasn't met, he would air-vac the child to a larger hospital. This is what followed.

Barbara was watching Phil Donahue one afternoon, while at the hospital visiting her grandchild. The topic was the AIDS virus. She asked Danny to have the hospital run the tests on the baby. Her son was irate that she would consider the possibility and angrier still that she would think he was gay or had used needles to contract this monster virus. I'm sure you can guess the rest of this story. The child, named Destiny, met with a grueling death. Danny's death followed, and two years later his wife passed away.

I listened to Barbara and felt the pain as she discussed each stage of this horrid situation that had touched and affected her entire family. When she finished, I asked, "Don't you wish you had had the information you now hold, concerning the violet Light/Presence of God, back then?" She answered affirmatively and quietly.

As for me, I was ready to go stand high atop a mountain and start yelling my lungs out to anyone who would listen to me, so you and your loved ones never need to experience such sadness and pain.

The Reluctant Messiah had stood upon the side of a hill in *Illusions* and yelled, "I QUIT." He was tired, remember, of feeding the people and fixing their lives. I needed to hear a story like Barbara's, to feel the compassion of an extension of myself, reminding me of those things I teach. I'm not here to fix, change, or save anyone. I'm not here to feed you, or fix your boo-boos, but by damn, I am here to teach you how to do what I do, empowering you with awareness of the Source that already lies within you. Barbara, used by God, changed my destiny. I don't want to quit. Because of her, countless more people will be touched and more books will be written.

I have an ego, but fortunately God knows it. Just as I was rejected by publishers "and would never give up" He, being rejected by me, was never going to give up, either. (He always wins.) He always has the ability to touch my heart, keeping me in harmony with the Divine Plan of my life.

What an incredible story, Gloria. I can only imagine the countless situations that you encounter. I think humanity has a false perception of their spirituality. We think if we "just get there," we'll have such an easy life. And yet, we listen to you and see how much you've struggled to get where you're going, how hard you have worked and continue to work. It shows us that once we attain that Conscious Oneness or Union, that we are not going to sit back and bask in the Light, never lifting a finger. To think that any longer is only sadly fooling ourselves.

You're right. Your life gets easier, in the sense that you no longer fear and worry, or even to "try and fix things," and you have unimaginable peace. Everything you need is provided. You experience exciting new and wonderful things that you've only heard from folklore, or read of.

But from my personal experience, I can only say that if you think you will become enlightened and have those to do your bidding—WRONG. You will serve others. Lucky for us, however, He is the Energy, the Will, the Driving Force, and the *Determination* to accomplish all that is asked of us.

My editor called one day and interrupted me while I was bringing wood into the garage. She was shocked that I use my healing hands for something so mundane. "Claire," I laughed, "I have become intimate with this wood. I loaded it into the truck, unloaded it, stacked it, and keep the garage filled. (It's a wonderful aerobic exercise.)" In Claire's mind,

I guess, she couldn't imagine me doing something so phys-ical if I do all these miraculous things. Every physical thing I can do . . . working out, pumping iron, mopping, vacu-uming, picking up dog poop from the yard—all make it possible for me to be physically stronger "to carry even more light." We must have the balance of the physical, or we will be useless as instruments.

I just don't think humanity ever "got it" before, Gloria. We judge ourselves that we're not "spiritual enough" if we don't meditate often enough. To hear that the physical is equally important to our spiritual growth certainly gives me (and others) a broader perspective.

I do have my kids' help with chores, and Kirk is a won-derful support in every way, but I'm not going to pass off any job I can do that will add to my strength of what I choose to do to help this world. Let them grow up and move out and get their own dogs to follow behind—their own yards to mow—this one is mine. I don't do the mun-dane out of martyrdom . . . I'm doing it to build some great spiritual (Popeye) muscles.

Good grief. When you say it like that, it makes me want to run out and just run, or do something . . . wash win-dows, rake, clean the garage and the top of the refrigerator . . . naaa . . . I don't want to go that far. Seriously, Gloria, this is incredible information. Who would have known that doing physical things like this had the ability to assist in our spiritual journey?

When I was growing up, my two elder sisters, Terry and Vicki, took piano lessons, and I remember my mom nag-ging at them to practice. She felt as if she was flushing money down the toilet. I, in third grade, began begging my mom to let me take piano lessons. Tired of wasting her money (and oh, ho hum, "breath"), she refused me. I continued to beg and after months of promising I would practice, she sent me for my first lesson.

Terry and Vicki had quit, which was good for me, because one piano and three girls would never have worked. Each night, and even before school, my mom would have to almost pry my fingers off the keys. I was addicted to the piano.

Seven years of lessons later, I lost my piano and was promised another one some day. The reason for sharing this story is because if Vicki and Terry had continued to practice daily, they would now still be able to play the piano. I walk into a room, after years of not practicing, and can still play familiar tunes. None of us became concert pianists, but that isn't the point of the story being told. The point is practice.

I receive calls, letters, and e-mails from people saying they do the exercises in my books, but some are unable to see the Light. *Continue your physical-spiritual workout, "exercising your faith" by practicing the Presence in every way on every day.* Mowing or meditation, anyone?

We, as humans, cannot "live the life of Christ" by willing or desiring to do so. Living the life isn't a matter of human will; everyone would like to live without negativity, fear, illness, or pain. Until God comes through you individually and makes Itself felt in your consciousness and experience, practice the techniques I teach. The achievements and results may take a day, a week, a month, or a year to realize, but once you do, your entire life is changed forever.

While in the Pacific Northwest doing healings, a woman sat in my chair. As I placed my hands upon her and closed my eyes, I saw the beauty of her soul. I knew she was a healer and carried more Light than I am able to do. When I told her she didn't need me, she cried. I had validated what

she had already known, but was unable (until that moment) to accept.

Spirit once asked me, "How will you feel when no one
needs you any longer?" I only had to think of the question
for a second before I returned my answer, "What a wonderful world we will live in."

Part Two

LEARNING HOW TO
SURRENDER JUDGMENT

17

I Have No Opinion

I need to ask you what you would like to do today. I promised you the time of your life on this journey, but I can't read your mind. (Actually, I'm very telepathic, but as soon as I tell people that, they get scared that I'm going to pick their brain. I would never do that, I promise.) To get you used to "asking for what you want" and feeling "comfortable doing so," ask me.

What are my choices, Gloria? Do you have any suggestions?

I can give you choices, of course. I can hire a massage therapist for you, I can give you a personal foot reflexology treatment, or I can give you a personal healing session and take you to "Bliss 101A." If you're getting bored with my stories, or just plain tired of me talking—I can give you alone time or the keys to my van. I could drive you around the area and introduce you to some of the nicest people you'd ever hope to meet. I could take you through a meditation, or I could promise you a miracle and I'd just hush for a minute. That's definitely a miracle whenever that happens.

Oh dear, those are some very enticing choices. Most all of them would be first-time experiences for me, too . . . and maybe, some day, I'll get another opportunity to take you up on some of them. But there is one thing I'd like to do, more than any of those, and if you don't mind, I'd really like to have a quiet day with you and continue listening to you talk. Would that be okay with you? Can we just sit out under the forested area of Fred and Dorothy's property and keep talking? That's what I'd rather do than anything.

AS YOU WISH.

A woman recently called from Atlanta, Georgia, seeking help. "I'm suicidal and severely depressed."

With a loving lilt in my voice I replied, "What a beautiful day to think of killing yourself."

Following my words was a very long pause, along with a giggle. "I never would have thought you'd use that kind of approach or response to my suicide threat." I responded, "Admit it. You like to be depressed because the pity party feels good."

Another long pause followed and she replied, "You certainly are unique in the way you handle this kind of situation." She had been depressed since high school. In minutes, she had been healed. She learned, also, whenever depression returned, to affirm, "What a beautiful day to feel depressed. Yippee Ki Yay—I'm a lucky girl to be depressed." We choose our emotions once we become aware.

Through a direct experience, I shared my past depression and thoughts of suicide with the woman. I had become friends with Nikki Fudge while she served a twelve-year sentence for prostitution and drug sales. She wrote, asking for spiritual guidance, and we ended up becoming best friends. She illustrated my self-published books, and I teasingly called her my "con artist."

After six years of her prison term, we received interstate-parole approval and she moved from California to Montana, living our dream as author/artist/inspirational speakers. However, Nikki soon became bored and annoyed with constant miracles and the retelling of them at workshops across the nation. I released her from the dream and she moved to Arizona to caretake an elderly woman.

I became depressed. I spent the entire day, after she drove away, sitting on my sofa and staring out at the mountains that surround our valley.

When Kirk returned from work that day, he asked how my day had been. "Not very good," I replied. "I thought about walking deep into the heart of the forest and digging a deep hole." Sighing heavily, I said, "But I couldn't think of a way to get the dirt in on top of me so no one would ever find me."

Gasping, Kirk remarked, "Oh, my God, Gloria. I'm concerned that you're entertaining thoughts of suicide."

Sarcastically I replied, "Right, Kirk. I'm going to physically walk into the woods, carrying a heavy shovel, dig into rock-hard dirt, and jump into a hole that might have worms or bugs in it. *I don't think so.* I'm just telling you how deep my despair is that Nikki chose to leave my life."

Remember? I'm so dang happy *all the time*—it just feels good to experience another emotion.

When we judge our feelings as bad or wrong, the discomfort continues. What we resist . . . persists. When we surrender judgment of anything, whether it's disease, poverty, poop-head relationships, or emotions, we reunite with the spiritual realm of goodness that has no opposite.

The shift in awareness of human good AND bad powers

to nonjudgment allows you to spiritually understand the lesson and discover spiritual goodness behind the appearance. In order to effectively silence the noisy mind, have no opinion.

I have no opinion concerning *(fill in the blank.)*

As an example, let's use the word 'alcohol.' That's a biggie in today's society. To those who are addicted and those who have judgments that it's "bad," be aware—you are setting the karmic law of human good and bad into motion. You experience illness, guilt, drunkenness, prison terms, frustration, traumas, and dramas.

Those who judge alcohol as "good" for reducing stress, achieving relaxation, alleviating modesty, and shyness also set the karmic law into motion.

Under spiritual law, alcohol is just alcohol. When you have no opinion, you neutralize karmic law and experience alcohol as just alcohol with no good or bad effects. You may, in fact, lose all taste for it . . . but with no human effort.

What I teach works. Surrender your judgments of illnesses, fears, hates, incompetence, selfishness, greed, food, and money.

Having no opinion silences the mind. If your mind has nothing good or bad to say about something or someone, you're at peace and the spiritual will manifest love in your outer world.

18
Here's to You

You cooked such a delicious brunch, Gloria, please allow
me to load the dishwasher while we keep talking. In fact,
since I'm standing, could I refill your coffee cup?

No thanks. In fact, how would you like me to make you
an iced mocha? And, what if I were to put the glass in your
hand, so we could raise them together in a cheer for life and
the miracle of it? How about if I asked whether you'd like
ice in that drink? How about if I offered three giant ice
cubes?

A woman from Iceland, the country known as "the land
of fire and ice" was visiting friends in Virginia. While there,
she heard about one of my books and made her way to
Montana to meet me personally and experience a healing.

While she sat at my kitchen table, she was talking about
her country and explained that beneath it hot, burning lava
flows. While she was educating me about Iceland and the
small fishing village she was from, she handed me a postcard. To this day, I continue to keep it on my refrigerator as
daily inspiration. If I ever feel fear, concerning a call I re-

ceive from a loved one or stranger, I look to the postcard and feel renewed in my strength to serve.

On September 30, an eruption occurred under Vatna-jokull, which set a tidal wave in motion. Glacial ice and water were carried over the area in a four- to five-meter-high wave, estimated at first to be thirty thousand cubic meters per second. The tsunami was headed toward this woman's village. A doorway to the sea, with protection from glacial rock on both sides of the opening, allowed villagers the possibility of being completely wiped out with the oncoming disaster.

God broke off three mountainous chunks of icebergs and completely sealed the opening to the village. Not one drop of water endangered the village. Only God would know what size ice cubes were necessary to do that, and I wonder when I look at this postcard how any of us could fret over any details of our lives. And yet we do. Daily.

Why? Because we've had more unanswered prayers than answered ones? Or is it because we feel so weak, helpless, and scared? Or we don't know where to start to fix our lives? Gosh, I can so easily relate to all of that.

I can only imagine, Glo-bug, how frustrated you've been to realize how simple healing is (and can be) and how to completely live a spiritual life when others continue to keep it mysterious or difficult. I'm sure countless judgments come with the territory of being a healer. "Who gave *YOU* the right to be a healer?" "Where in the Bible does it say to keep an open mind?" I could go on and on with the fears and concerns our society probably still has when you attempt to share this message. In fact, I have to be honest . . . it wasn't so long ago that I was judging people, just like you, myself.

I'm not throwing stones or passing blame, and I don't

have the answer whether it's religions that want to keep people frightened or if it's just the mass state of consciousness that terrorizes us from opening ourselves to the Presence of God. Maybe He's gotten a bad name for Himself for allowing mankind their creations. What I do know is that every person on this planet should have the ability and opportunity to hear the simplicity of what you teach. Then they, themselves, can choose to practice the Presence and see the direct results or to remain at the level they are and enjoy the traumas and dramas. Also, Gloria, I promise not to be part of the world's "problem" anymore.

We dismiss our power. I speak from experience. The power flowing through me, on occasion, has frightened me.

A 4:00 A.M. telephone call came in, advising me that a family member had had a heart attack. She would be going in for surgery, but there was a great chance she wasn't going to make it. I sat crying in the dark on the sofa, drinking coffee and chain-smoking. All of a sudden I had the realization, "I call myself a healer and if I can't help my loved one, I'll never again call myself that—and I'll never attempt to help anyone else. And I know this is ego talking—but I don't care . . . *because that's just exactly how I feel.*" I went and lay upon my bed and said, "God, use me," and I had my hiney electrocuted so strongly . . . that I was nearly knocked out of bed. However, I knew she would live and be okay. The following day, I sent three red roses to the hospital, along with a card that said, "Trust that God can fix anything, even a broken heart." Three days later, she was released and hasn't had another problem since.

The healing I just spoke of was an absentee healing, meaning I was used as an instrument across the miles.

Before I tell the following story, I'd like to make you aware of Kirk's high threshold of pain. When he moved myself and the two younger children to Montana, he was adding on another bedroom and bathroom to the existing home.

I was out back one morning as he was working on the roof of the addition and I heard him say, "I shouldn't have done that." I raised my hand to shield my eyes from the sun behind him and asked, "What did you do?"

"I hit my thumb with the hammer," he responded.

Only moments later, without cursing, he said, "Oh, I shouldn't have done that either." As before, I questioned, "What did you do now?"

"I hit it again."

Kirk and I had attended my friend Nikki's Halloween party, and during the drive home, he was driving very slowly. Thinking he was tired, I offered to drive. He said he was fine; however, I noticed that he not only drove slowly, but also on the shoulder of the road. Since we live in the Bitterroot Valley, here in Montana, and we have so many deer casualties, I was presupposing that he was being cautious.

Oh, no, God . . . please don't tell me that this is headed where I think it is. Okay. Okay. Okay. I'll hush and just listen . . . ohhhh . . . gosh, I just don't like what I'm feeling of where this conversation is going.

When I awoke the following morning, Kirk wasn't in bed with me. He never leaves me sleeping, but I thought that he was unable to sleep and didn't want to disturb me after our late night.

I made breakfast and we ate, and he offered to drive D.W. to paintball practice. He went out to start the car and warm it, and as he returned to the kitchen, he sat down and grabbed his heart. "I'm hurting pretty bad," he said. I knew if Kirk was validating pain, he was hurtin' for certain.

I began rubbing my hands together and as I was walking around the table to get to him, I asked, "Do you want me to call 9 1 1?" (This is "God-emergency backup," in my opinion.)

"No," he responded. I placed my hands on him, intuitively guided. My right (power) hand on his forehead, which elevates consciousness quickly. My left hand upon his heart.

Being empathic, I could literally feel the electrical, violent waves ripping through his heart. I was taking deep breaths and turning my face to the right to exhale as quickly as I could, which bleeds off excess energy very quickly.

I felt the entire process that was occurring with Kirk as I felt his left arm and armpit go numb. I continued to silently chant, "Peace, peace, peace be with me." (I'll ask for nothing more, but I'll settle for nothing less.)

"Peace, peace, peace be with me" is the calming agent that continues to keep me focused and unafraid as I meet frightening experiences with strangers . . . as well as loved ones, because it's difficult at times to remain neutral when you're working on someone so emotionally close.

Only minutes passed and Kirk patted my left hand and said, "It's okay, now, you can let go." Still feeling the erratic energy, I replied, "No. It's not okay yet."

Only a few more minutes passed and I felt that the situation was no longer life-threatening. Kirk then shared that he had a heart attack while at Nikki's party, thus the reason for his slow-driving behavior on the way home. He had been drained from the pain. Another heart attack occurred earlier that morning and that's why he'd left me alone in bed.

Literally, after only minutes, Kirk—acting as if he'd tripped on a shoestring and stumbled for a second—got into the car and drove D.W. to paintball, as planned. It wasn't until he drove away that I felt complete panic. I felt completely stupid for allowing him to get behind the wheel of a car. I was pacing when our daughter Jaime arrived and I told her what had occurred. From an outsider's perspective, if Kirk was able to get behind the wheel, then perhaps it wasn't really a heart attack we'd been dealing with. But it was.

Oh, Gloria, I'm so very sorry that you had to experience this with your husband, but do you even begin to realize how your teachings from that day can affect the lives of others? I think most people, whenever they get a twinge in the chest area, immediately get frightened. With your training, fears can be reduced and practical application applied. Again, I'm so sorry that you had to learn this one through direct experience, but I'm also so grateful that you did.

I know. There's that ol' "good or bad, who's to say" teaching that we can remember as we meet uncomfortable situations throughout our lives. As a healer, I can't have opinions. I must remain neutral and I'm also totally ineffective if I feel fear. In the moment I was needed, I was neutral and unafraid. I did what I had to do. When this or other situations arise, we, as healers, must begin immediately rubbing our hands together, silently asking for peace. Later, we have permission to fall apart, because by then the Light/Christ is already on the scene and the healing will occur.

We live in a physical world, under karmic and man-made laws. Until our consciousness is heightened, we are still subject to the experiences of this world. Taking physical precautions is not denying our spiritual nature or truth. We can believe something with all our heart, but it isn't the wishing or hoping that will ever make it manifest. The truth and experiences I share are direct. I may have read something many times, loving the beauty of the words, but until I demonstrate it, those pretty words aren't going to do anything.

I would love it if I were "on" twenty-four hours a day, connected directly and strongly to the Source. That continues to happen, as my consciousness rises, but the demonstrations, again, are the witness and result of where my state of consciousness rests. It must be *each person's responsibility* to open themselves to the Light. We, as healers, are not here to fix, change, or save anyone. (No, not even our knights in shining armor.) We can share our Light with all who reach out to us, but that will only give a temporary state "of better humanhood." That isn't the purpose of my teachings.

Oops. Sorry. I got carried away, trying to make a point. Kirk rested on Saturday and Sunday. On Monday he went to work, and at 7:00 A.M. I felt the pressure in my heart center and my left arm went numb again. I called and asked if he was okay and he said, "Yes."

"Liar, liar, pants on fire. You just had another one, didn't you?"

"Yes . . ."

Kirk's employer had him driven to the emergency room, but all the ensuing tests revealed no damage to his heart and no scar tissue.

I, however, knew that Spirit was preparing me for more individuals whom I would be asked to assist. It's always been like that. If I travel to a city to do private healings, I have found that if the first person has cancer or neck problems, or whatever the situation may be, the entire day will be spent working with those issues. Because Kirk had experienced a heart attack, I knew what would be forthcoming.

A local woman called during my dinner hour. She, too, was experiencing a heart attack. She called me instead of 9 1 1 (which I wouldn't recommend). I left my dinner and family and took her through the process, also. Medical tests revealed no heart damage and no scar tissue.

You know how, when a person gets emergency medical training, or CPR training, and they come across an accident on the highway, they feel more prepared to offer assistance? It's the same with the spiritual healing you're teaching us, isn't it? If we are aware how to assist ourselves and loved ones through this painful process, quickly, while medical teams are on their way to help, we won't feel as helpless and hopeless. This is all so perfect. But, Gloria, are we ever going to be given more than we can handle with our present state of awareness?

You won't be given basics and asked to go heal the multitudes of cancer, heart attacks, or serious, life-threatening situations. Like me, you may not be aware of how expanded your consciousness is until you find yourself in the actual experience and "doing it," even before you knew you could.

I'm sharing my human vulnerabilities and fears with you, to make you aware I wasn't always confident. People admire my gift and wish for one like it. In my speaking and teaching, I share countless, remarkable, uplifting events that have occurred. But I never felt safe enough, until now, to tell you some of my personal fears associated with my gift.

I didn't want to blindly trust, especially not if I was to be a spiritual leader or teacher for masses of people. I admitted that I feared my power and surrendered. I stopped "trying to figure it out" and watched as the Presence continued to work through me—whether I meditated or made it a point to open myself to be used.

It's a beautiful feeling to experience the Presence, randomly throughout the day . . . inwardly smiling, knowing that someone who has the ability to redeem and renew a person's spirit and soul has come into the realm of my state of consciousness. The way it feels begins as a tremendously warm glow around my entire head. The glow actually feels as if it's flowing throughout my body. Sometimes I feel electrical jerks or shocks in my body, and then I smile and my heart warms, knowing someone just experienced a miracle through me.

I know you are afraid of your power also. But it's my hope that in sharing what happens in the evolution of man's mind, as it becomes purified and healed from the simple technique taught in *Go Within or Go Without,* you will have a greater understanding than I did in my beginning years.

I'm being honest, Gloria. I was skeptical. I had read your other writings, some of your spiritual columns, and almost even made it to one of your workshops. But the skeptic in me resisted. I wanted to hope you were what you were professing to be, but I had a lot of doubts. I'm so glad I was *wrong.*

I *love* skeptics. Years ago, an elderly gentleman sat in my healing chair. I asked, "Is there anything in particular you need help with, or would you like an overhaul?" Giggling, I said, "It comes highly recommended."

In a gruff voice, he responded, "I don't even want to be here, but my daughter forced me to come. The medical world hasn't been able to help me and I've hurt for years . . . and I sure as hell don't think you can do anything to help me."

I smiled and said, "Sir, that's okay, because all you have to do is nothing and all I'm going to do is love you more than you've ever been loved before in your life."

After twenty minutes, I opened my eyes and removed my hands from the man's body. I said, "Sir, because we're One and I don't feel any more pain in my body, there's no more pain in yours, right?"

"Right, right," he said slowly and in awe.

"Well, I'm pretty sure I got all of it dissolved, but if not and you feel pain resurfacing—I'd like to make you aware that I can do this as easily long distance as I can in the physical. I do long distance healings at 6:00 A.M., noon, and 10:00 P.M. every night. So if you ever feel pain, all you have to do is think about me, and I'll send love across the miles."

In a tone of deep appreciation, he said, "I'm going to think about you at 2, 4, 6, 8, and 10:00 P.M.—in fact, I'm going to think about you every single second for the rest of my life."

I smiled and said, "And I love skeptics."

All those things that we, as humans, worry about and fear are simply passing events. In the bigger picture, a Divine Mind holds each of us safely and securely. And when you find yourselves doubting, as this man did, think back to the fishing village I spoke of as I began telling these stories. If you ever think that your individual life is a temporary mess, you are herein reminded that in spiritual reality, it's in Divine Order, and when you raise your consciousness and drink in life to its fullest . . . no one will have to ask you, "Would that be one ice cube, or two?"

19
You Just Believe

Okay. Tag. You're it. I've been guiding where the conversations go for more than twenty-four hours now; it's your turn. You choose what you'd like to hear about.

Thanks. Call me psychic, but you're doing that just to get me used to "asking for what I want" and "receiving," aren't you? I'm startin' to figure you out . . . Everything is teaching us when we're reading your works, or listening to your words. You're a pretty smart cookie, I'd say. And you do it so sneakily, too.

All right. Heavy sigh. I guess if I chose to head you in some direction that I most needed to hear, it would probably be along the lines of learning to accept physical or spiritual gifts and different ways that love can affect our lives. Like you say, I'm becoming more conscious and being clear by asking for what I want. So with that in mind, Globug . . . go for it. Lay it on me; hit me with your best shot.

Well, since I talked so much about Kirk, I feel like I'm on a roll, here, and if you don't mind, I'd like to share a loving experience concerning him. He gifts me every day with a listening ear, arms to be held in, and support financially, physically, emotionally, and spiritually. It was actually through marrying Kirk that I realized *I was willing to have it all.* And by golly, I deserve it, too.

Years ago, he'd asked me to write a song for him, (and to sing it for him too—big mistake. I can't sing). So I fulfilled his wish, had a friend sing it, and gave a recorded cassette to him in his Christmas stocking. He took that gift to work to share with his coworkers.

At the end of the day, he said he was feeling *deep love* for me as he walked to his vehicle. He felt gratitude and believed *he had everything.* Later that evening, he told me that when he had that thought, he inwardly laughed. He said that reality faced him as he was getting into an old, silver Isuzu pickup, wearing a denim jacket that he has resewn twice to give it an extended life. Anyone who would have heard him say "he had everything," when the physical world contradicted those words, would have thought Kirk was crazy.

Prosperity comes in more forms than physical dollars. To quote Kirk concerning the above experience, "Whether you wear denim or a shield of steel, it's what's in and felt with the heart that makes a knight in shining armor."

I've told others for years, "Don't give me a gift unless you don't mind that I give it away five minutes after it has been given to me." In the past, for example, I had been given an expensive necklace, and when the next person I met remarked of its beauty, I removed the jewelry from my neck in that moment and placed it around hers.

A woman from Alaska gifted me with an (ugly) coffee mug that embellished "Alaska" on one side and "Gloria" on the other. She said she'd heard that it's difficult for me to keep gifts, and if I ever wanted to give it away, at least I'd have to find another Gloria to give it to.

She limited my giving, until I became aware one day that I could fill it with money and give it to someone who wasn't named Gloria. I handed the gift to the woman in need, and said, "Your cup runneth over with love and abundance." Gloria isn't just my name, it's also the reference, "Glory to God in the highest." And that gift is available to everyone, no matter what their name is.

I LOVE PEOPLE. Those I've physically touched have been a gift to me, as well. Those I've reached, however, although they love my attitude and ability to be so down-to-earth, tend to forget there's a Gloria, JUST LIKE THEM, underneath all that love.

Do you mean to tell me that you EVER have a bad day? No way . . . this I've got to hear.

While cooking during the holidays, I spilled my entire pumpkin pie mix all the way across the kitchen and into the oven. I burned one entire pan of homemade dinner rolls. I didn't cook my marshmallow fudge long enough and we had to use it as sauce over ice cream. My daughter spilled the 7 Up salad (in its liquid stage) on the floor. It was a day that everything I touched turned to poop.

I had made a separation by saying, "I have so many things to do," and I was depending on limited, human/ Gloria-do-it-yourself power, rather than allowing the unlimited God power to do it for me.

It's when we don't "have time" that we must make time to reawaken us to a conscious realization of our Oneness with God. When we do, we don't spill pies, burn dinner rolls, or undercook our fudge. When we hurt (on any level), feel fear, know confusion or despair, we close our eyes and watch as the inner (violet) Light dissolves the belief in separation from our Source and heals our individual mind, restoring right action.

**Sorry, Glo-bug, but I'm feeling that thankfulness sensa-
tion again that even you can "forget to plug in" or "open
yourself to the Presence" even at your present level of
awareness. I don't think you understand, at all, how important it is to share your humanness with people. You
probably do that, on purpose, just so we don't put you on a
pedestal. Oh, God, I'm right, aren't I?**

I am human, and I definitely want to keep it that way, if
you don't mind. In my executive secretary career, before I
had children, I was being interviewed for a job. My résumé
was confident to say the least. I could type or take short-
hand at 120 words per minute, each. Those gifts opened
any door I needed to have opened.

One line of my résumé said, "Because of my organiza-
tional abilities, along with the speed, I am able to generate a
great quantity of work in a quality unsurpassed by many
other secretaries.

The man interviewing me asked, "Can you walk on
water, too?" I smiled and said, "Yes . . . if it's not too deep."
Of course, I got the job.

**You're so good to people, Gloria. I'm a stranger to you,
and you completely open your life to me and help me feel
important, as if I'm your best friend. How do you do that?
It's so difficult to think of people opening themselves the
way you do, extending your heart to the entire world. Can
you tell me a story of how you mix miracles and meatloaf,
just any ol' story of how you might stop what you're doing
just to have a spontaneous miracle occur?**

I was interrupted from holiday baking during the year of
all my screw-ups when Sandy and her darling four-year-
old, Miss Molly, dropped by. While we sat at the kitchen

table, having hot apple cider and cookies fresh from the oven, Sandy brought up the subject of healing.

Well, by golly, Miss Molly took the opportunity of joining fully in the adult conversation by telling me she'd been hurt (for the third time) at the day care center. It seems that her little elbow had been pulled out of joint three times with the children pulling on her arms as if she were a little wishbone.

Miss Molly asked me if I would heal her arm. I invited her upon my lap, closed my eyes, and felt the energy block up near her armpit. I felt as the block dissolved and watched as (violet) Light filled my entire inner vision. I opened my eyes and asked if she'd seen the Light and she replied, "Oh yes, the whole room is purple." Miss Molly's arm no longer hurt.

You only asked for one, but I like this story, too. I think it's so important to share. I attended a gymnastics recital for Danielle. Following her performance, a little girl ran, cartwheeled, and flipped (without spotters). As her feet hit the floor, she sprained her ankle. Alligator tears flowed down her cheeks (embarrassed, I'm sure) as she hobbled to her mother who just happened to be sitting behind me.

I could overhear her crying and my inner voice urged me to help her. I resisted only for a moment and turned around, looking into her eyes. "If I rub my hands together, they get very warm, and if you'd allow me to put them on your ankle, I could help it feel better." I asked the child, not the mother, "Would you allow me to do this?" Without speaking and with the tears still flowing, she trusted me and nodded her head, "Yes."

I placed my hands on her ankle and felt six immediate "shifts." She said, "My ankle doesn't hurt anymore" and I responded, "I know . . ."

On the way home from that gymnastics meet, it was "dark/thirty" and I had "the pedal to the metal." I was driving over 75 mph when my inner voice said, "Slow down, there's a deer ahead." I removed my foot from the accelerator and dropped to 45. A second message followed, "Slow down, there's a deer ahead." As I stepped on the brake and dropped to 35, I blinked my bright lights on . . . just as the deer's head turned and his gold eyes shined in my headlights.

The deer was standing broadside in my lane of travel. Had I not listened to my heart, I would have killed Danielle and myself that night—and the deer, too.

As I said, we live in a physical world and I believe this realm is as important as the spiritual. My world is the mundane of daily cleaning and cooking, mixed with the miraculous. But I still clean toilets, make messes, and am a miracle worker on the side. I think it's important for me to explain the mystical side of life, which you will experience as your consciousness rises. However, you still live in a physical world, and remember? We must continue to use seatbelts, rather than falsely trusting that God will save us (if they are mere words, rather than a heightened state of awareness).

I enjoy your stories, Gloria; please don't apologize that you're telling too many. In fact, I think it's cute that you call yourself a third-generation motormouth; but listen here, girlie—you're right on the edge of being critical of yourself, rather than being funny. If you're not careful, I'll have you following your own advice from *Go Within* and you'll be saying ten nice things about yourself to me.

Without a doubt, love is your motivation. I can hear it, as well as feel it while you're speaking (or writing). I'd like to hear another story, concerning a child.

Aye Aye (and a respectful salute). Point well taken. I will not be critical of myself any longer (or at least not around you).

A little eight-year-old, Scott, felt the love you speak of as well, when he heard me speak in 1995 . . . the first night I went public with the message.

Scott had lost his eyeglasses three times in only a few weeks and his parents, tired of repurchasing the glasses, brought him to me for a private healing. As he sat tall and proud in my healing chair, he told me that he had used the information I gave the audience that night to heal their dying family dog. He went on to explain that the tiny pin-points of white light, in his inner vision, "bring him typed messages he can read." He said, "I call the white lights 'Comets.' "

I asked Scott to ask his "Comets" if his eyesight would be healed after our first visit and without pausing, he replied, "The Comets just told me that I'll have to see you one more time and then I won't need glasses any longer." I asked if his Comets had a message for me.

Once again, without hesitation, he said, "Gloria, the Comets tell me that if you will continue to help people every day, they will give you a reward." I asked what kind of reward that would be and Scott replied, "Freedom." (Wouldn't freedom, from the worldly belief of dual powers of good and bad, be a wonderful gift? Freedom from all fear and all "appearances of imperfection"?)

Very quietly, Scott said, "Gloria, the Comets just told me to tell you that you need to start doing this faster, though." I asked if his Comets would teach me how to be faster and with such authority from this eight-year-old boy, he heavily sighed and remarked, "You just believe . . . "

Well, alrighty then. I do . . . I do . . . I do-o-o-o believe in miracles.

20
Memories of Love

This day has absolutely flown by. Lounging around the house, sharing miracle stories and conversations has certainly made me feel serene. Wouldn't it be wonderful if people could place their attention upon these beautiful things in life, rather than in the next "guess what went wrong today" situation? I know you need to get ready to speak this evening; how about if you shower first and I'll make lunch with whatever's in the refrigerator that you brought as groceries, and I'll ask if Fred and Dorothy would like to join us.

That would be wonderful. Thanks . . . I'll see you shortly.

Holy guacamole—you make wonderful Mexican food. These rolled chicken tacos with sour cream and guacamole are probably the best I've ever eaten. I'm sorry Fred and Dorothy couldn't join us. I didn't know they were expecting guests and had other plans for today. But I sure do give thanks for this meal made with loving hands.

Ya know, Gloria, while you were showering, I noticed your face on a newspaper over on Dorothy's bookcase. It

was one of your earlier *Open Line* newspaper columns and I couldn't help but read it and I found it so fascinating. Would you mind if I read it aloud to you?

No, in fact, that would be fun. I used to have Nikki read everything aloud to me that I'd written so I could hear the flow of it. When she heard that you were joining me on this trip, she laughed and asked, "You're not going to make your guest read a full manuscript on the four-hour drive like you made me do with *Go Within* before it went to press, are you?" Bless her heart. She read four straight hours, on that mountainous road . . . twisting and turning . . . and I can't help but chuckle at how carsick she got. (See. I'm not always nice, am I?)

Ah-hem . . . okay, here goes.

Years ago, I attended Danielle's final elementary school concert. I sat on the top row of the bleachers, as usual, for two reasons: (1) To support my back against the brick wall, and (2) so no one would see the tears in my eyes. Whenever I see my kids in an activity such as singing, band, a parade, or anything they're doing in public, I cry. Tears of pride, and remember? The Presence of God.

Other people's children can have the same effect on me. I remember one morning in particular, when I drove my son to first grade. A child wanting to cross the street, waited courteously for me to go first. Instead, I stopped and motioned to him to feel safe enough to cross. He jumped from the curb and ran across the street. He jumped up on the curb, turned toward me, bowed, and said "Thank you." I began crying.

In fact, I cried all the way home. I couldn't understand my tears. What was wrong with me? The child merely said "Thank you," although the bow took me by surprise.

When I got home, I silently asked, "My God, what's the

matter with me? Why can't I stop crying? My inner voice said, "You felt My Presence." And so I did. And so do you, at times.

I was called upon, several years ago, to fly to Hershey, Nebraska, to help a dying thirteen-year-old boy. Two months after I left, he passed away because of pneumonia. I wrote a letter to his family. When people call me for guidance or healing for their fears, I always tell them, "I'll walk each step with you. Keep in touch and share your "happily-ever-after," and please take care . . . I care . . .

Letters such as the following aren't easy for me to write, but I wanted to share what I said. I didn't have the "right" words to say, so I let my heart do the talking.

Dearest Vivian, Darrell, and Miss Becky,

It was two weeks ago today that I received the call about Brian. Please forgive me for not responding sooner, but I wanted to give you some time before I popped back into your life again. I needed the time, myself, to understand and feel all the feelings concerning the situation.

Brian has just become the fifth finger, on one hand, in counting the times in thirteen years of me being a healer, that passing was the result. Let me tell you, it doesn't get any easier no matter how many fingers I can hold up in re-membrance. I could tell myself a bazillion times that good stands behind all appearances, but in this instance or any like it—they are just words.

I was in your family's life for only three days. I watched you walk into the room and look down upon your son, asking if there was anything you could get or do for him. I watched Darrell sit at the foot of the couch and tenderly place his hand on Brian's leg and look at him with love eyes. These are memories of your love that will forever remain with Brian (and me. Love never dies—we take it with us).

Brian wasn't just a kid that had cancer who needed my

help. I told you how many times he reminded me of my own son. I looked upon Brian as if he were mine. I didn't feel helpless or hopeless at any point, no matter what the medical world was telling you . . . so you must imagine my surprise when I received the call that the cancer was dissolving, but that pneumonia took him.

In all the past situations of a person's passing, I wanted "to give up." I don't like the human caring and compassion that I feel . . . followed with the feeling of failure or "if I could just get my consciousness high enough, this would never need to happen." This case is unlike all others, because I don't feel like a failure. Because of Brian, I am more inspired than ever to send my writings across the world so we (all of humanity) can dissolve cancer and other "hopeless" diseases from the mass consciousness so these situations never touch anyone's life again.

I will always hold Brian in loving tribute on stage or in writings when I share that in the past, whenever things didn't work out according "to my plan," I wanted to give up. I didn't want to play any more if God wasn't going to play by my rules. Remember when everyone encouraged me to go to Nebraska, sharing it was in Divine Order? I, as Gloria, believed that meant that Brian would be healed . . . dazzling the doctors and going on to live a full and complete life. God's plan taught me once again not only to surrender expectations, but also how to see that I've grown beyond the "give up and never play again" stage I felt so comfortable with.

I'm printing this letter on rainbow stationery today, because the clouds have lifted . . . Brian no longer needs medication (or a healer at his side) to numb his pain. The rainbow is a symbol of Christ, to me, and appears often when I'm seeking a human fulfillment of needing to know I'm still on the right track.

Vivian, Darrell, and Miss Becky/Beauty . . . not a day has passed since we met that I haven't included you in my prayers. No words from me can ease the heartache you've felt for ten months, as well as losing a beloved son (and brother). I don't want even to pretend I have any of the right words to ease your pain because I am feeling it right along with you.

People may be in awe of the miracles that occur through me, but I'd like to make them also aware of the human pain and suffering I feel right along with them. I have not ascended above the human scene to stand apart, but instead, I carry the burden right along with them. Maybe I will never rise above that level in this dimension. First of all so that it reminds me of why I'm here and why God needs to use me, but also to remain connected to the human senses so I can testify to the needs of His Glory, Truth, and infinite Love.

I was never to be used for Brian or anyone to heal the physical. I was merely to open the consciousness to God. "It," in Its infinite awareness does fulfill perfection. Most often, that means a physical healing/miracle . . . and I'm sure that just as soon as I surrender my judgment of this situation, I'll have better clarity of His Divine Plan.

If you need to talk, please call. If I need to talk, I'll call . . . I love you all with my whole, great big heart.

I believe this letter speaks for itself, but I'd like to share an experience I had while in Spokane, Washington. I know that death isn't "bad" because I've been there, done that. I've had personal experiences, visions, and dreams that attempt to assist my conscious mind to spiritually understand and accept.

The experience involved a mother, Cindy, and her teenage daughter, Erica. As they entered the healing room, Cindy sat in my canvas-back chair to be first.

As usual, I asked whether there was something in particular she'd like help with . . . or an overhaul, which came highly recommended. She replied that her husband had recently died, in peace, and assured that wherever he was . . . he was in peace. However, she wasn't. As I approached Cindy to stand behind her, I was rubbing my hands briskly together. Just before I laid hands upon her head, I stated, "Well, why don't we just invite Frank's spirit to be with us today and perhaps any one of the three of us could share the message."

I no sooner placed my hands on Cindy's head, closed my eyes, when Frank was in my inner vision. He stood before me, with a Bud Light in his hand and said, "Here's to you—tell her." I silently listened as he continued to talk and share things he wanted me to tell Cindy and Erica. I just couldn't do it. My human personality resisted all that I was seeing and hearing.

I told Frank telepathically, "I just can't do it." Three times, he repeated, "Please, Gloria. Trust your thoughts and share these words. They're so important for her to hear."

James Van Praugh has a best-seller, *Talking with Heaven*. I haven't read it yet, but I've seen him a couple of times on talk shows. I know that what he says he can do, he can do. I have no doubts.

Getting messages from souls in other dimensions on a personal level holds a great responsibility . . . or at least for me, and in this particular situation.

Just before I took my hands away from Cindy's heart, Frank suggested that I ask Cindy and Erica, "Why February was so important."

I didn't want to do it and shared my fears with the woman and child. I attempted "to test her," by asking, first of all, if Frank drank Bud Light. She affirmed he did. I then felt safe enough to tell her that he offered it in a cheer of,

"Here's to you." She affirmed again that he did that quite often.

She affirmed each verbal love offering from him. When I asked, "Why was February so important," she and Erica got teary. Cindy told me that it was February 14, and though Frank was so ill, he had called the florist and had flowers delivered for both of them.

He hadn't been sleeping well and on this day, he took a two-and-a-half-hour nap. When he awoke, he told Cindy that he'd seen the man bring the flowers. She negated him by saying, "You couldn't possibly have seen the man, Frank, you were asleep in the back bedroom."

He assured her, "Not only did I see the man deliver the flowers, but I can tell you from start to finish what the movie was about that you were watching while I napped." He concluded, "And I also saw God's Divine Plan . . . I was fully aware of everything while in that state of Consciousness."

As I was giving Cindy the final heart-to-heart goodbye hug, Frank appeared in my inner vision again. Three times he said, "*Please feel me*" to Cindy. I told her, "This is Frank hugging you and these are the words he is saying: "*I will guide you, but you must listen to, and trust, your thoughts.*" Before we released from the hug, he laughed and asked me to tell her, "*And I'm going to send you a man . . .*"

Cindy laughed, knew, and believed this was truly Frank speaking. For the last two weeks before he died, he continually spoke of sending her a man. It was an awesome experience for all of us that afternoon.

When I "died," I, too, was fully conscious of everything going on simultaneously in the universe. I could see that my physical body was dead, but the individuality of me was alive and well. (Because consciousness never dies.)

If I know all this, why would I feel so badly that Brian's soul chose to depart this dimension? Humanly, I've still bought into the belief system that it's a great loss to "lose" a loved one. We like our loved ones "with skin on." As we spiritually grow, perhaps we'll believe and celebrate the graduation from this plane of existence to the next level of understanding. I'm not at that point, however, but I do know that when you die—you don't "go" anywhere, except to the invisible level, which our mortal eyes cannot see. Brian's and Frank's spirits are with us and if we'll just trust, as Frank suggested, those who have a broader picture of what's going on, they will guide us well.

When D.W. was little, I couldn't keep his clothes on him. He'd run around nude and had no embarrassment whatsoever. One morning, he peeked through a knothole in the fence and saw children. He said, "Hi kids." They asked him what his name was and he replied, "D.W./big boy/buster-butt, Herbert." They, of course, laughed and said, "What a silly name and you're naked, too."

He never ran around naked again. I told my (first) husband, "It must have been how Adam and Eve felt. They didn't 'know' they were naked until someone told them." Looking through a knothole and seeing a limited view is what we humans do concerning most of what we experience in daily living.

As I stated earlier, "I'm not asking you to think like me. I'm just sharing more mind-expanding experiences and possibilities as we, together, journey back to the Heart of God.

Gloria, my goodness. What a wonderful column that was. Even now, since I've read it twice, it's something I'd like to read again and again. You talk about surrendering judgment, and these situations are such biggies for humanity. I hope you're going to have more time this weekend to talk about death and dying. It's so important for the world to have a spiritual understanding of all this.

I'd be happy to. It is no accident that you found and read that column out of all the ones I've ever written. I'm not even surprised that you would continue to read that column once you realized that pain had touched a child's life. I remember your reaction from yesterday, and you're such a tenderhearted bear, I'm proud of you that you could feel that fear and do it anyway. I also *knew intuitively* you had lost someone close to you and haven't found completion with it. God's a smart Hummer, for sure, isn't He? I **know** why you're on this journey with me.

You don't have to tell me, whether it was a child you lost, a mate, a friend, or a loved one—or whether it's "you" you've lost. You can hold that information privately . . . I won't pry.

I'll be reciting a fairy tale in tonight's message and I believe it will touch your heart. I trust you're going to find awareness and completion tonight for the pain you've carried.

Let me stand on this stool, so we can more comfortably hug. Come here, sweetie, put your arms around me. It's okay if you cry. I will too. You've carried this alone for so very long. *(Heavy sigh.)* I'm so very sorry that you didn't know, until now, how loved you are.

Why don't you take your turn in the shower now, and I'll open myself to the Light so I'll be an effective speaker. I haven't told you, by the way, where we're going tonight. I'm speaking to a large group of people who have lost loved ones and haven't found peace in their passing. You don't need to be afraid; if you'll put your hand in my hand, I will be your friend.

21
Angels Walk Among Us
(Saturday Night Speech)

Good evening ladies and gentlemen. I come before you, to stand behind you . . . to tell you something of which I know nothing about. Next Thursday, which is Good Friday, there will be a men's meeting that only ladies can attend. Admission is free—pay at the door. Sit on the floor and we'll discuss the four corners of the round table.

With all of the fast talkers, double talkers, and smooth talkers out there, is there any reason *why* we're so confused?

A guest I brought to Spokane threatened me today. If I didn't stop berating myself, I would be asked to say ten nice things about myself. I believe that's a very good idea, about now, especially since I opened this inspirational speech the way I did tonight. But, rather than ten, I think three would be acceptable since it's only a first warning. Three nice things about me are:

1. I'm honest. If I am telling you a story and during it, I correct myself, "Well, actually that happened in Los Angeles, not Denver," it's not because I'm neurotic, although I can be that too. I'm doing so to establish a trust

within you, that to the best of my ability, everything I say is true from my perception of the experience.

2. I'm a person of my word. I mean what I say and I say what I mean.

3. I'm fun to play with.

Since my time with you this evening is limited to twenty minutes, I think it's important to gift you with information that is valuable . . . just in case you don't learn it from my writings. You are a spiritual being. Your nature is giving. You give and give, and when you're tired, you give some more. However, we must first "have it," before we give it, or we will soon find ourselves lacking in finances or health.

When you rub your hands together, this "turns on the energy." Your eyes are the windows to the soul and the fastest way to get energy into the body. And remember the body can heal, but it needs energy to do so.

For two to ten minutes, place your hands over your eyes. Place the palms themselves over the eyes, with the fingers upon your forehead (third eye). You may or may not see the violet Light with your hands in this position. Sometimes I do. Sometimes I don't. Regardless, if you can't actually see the Light in your inner vision, you will feel the warmth from your hands. This exercise dissolves negativity you've taken on during the day, expands your consciousness, and elevates your energy field. Although you need to do this for only a few minutes, you can do it longer if you choose—because no one has ever over overdosed on love.

To give you an example of the difference this can make in your life, I will share a personal experience.

When my daughter Danielle was celebrating her four-teenth birthday, I allowed her to invite eight girls for a sleep-over. With that many children, in such a small home, we had them lie upon the floor, like sardines, in their sleeping bags. They awakened Kirk and me at 2:00 A.M., having caterpillar races on the kitchen floor.

The following morning, I was making breakfast pizzas for our guests. The smoke alarm went off, and one of Danielle's little friends started shaking, and in a very nervous voice she cried, "Oh my God, what's . . . that . . . sound?" Danielle, in a tone of disbelief that the child "didn't know" said, "It's just the smoke alarm—doesn't your mom set hers off every time she cooks?"

I was embarrassed. After I delivered all the children to their respective homes, I returned and sprayed oven cleaner and thought, "While that's dissolving, I'll clean the refrigerator and small freezer." When I finished that task, I cleaned and defrosted the big freezer and rotated all the food.

I went to the pantry for something and saw *that pigs must live here,* so and I cleaned and organized it. The mess above the washer and dryer was cleaned, too, as well as the fan and light above the table.

Around the kitchen I went, cleaning every cupboard and drawer, vacuuming the flour bin and cleaning the microwave, until I found myself back at the dirty stove where it all began. All the yuck had dripped down into the broiler and onto the floor, so I cleaned the oven hood, the stovetop, the oven itself, and the broiler; then I mopped and waxed the kitchen floor.

From the moment I stepped into the kitchen to make breakfast, until it was completely cleaned, I had spent eighteen hours. I was so tired I could have cried. Rather than going to bed and tossing and turning, I went to the "love" seat (where I do long distance healings), rubbed my hands, and put them over my eyes for fifteen minutes.

Da da da da da da . . . CHARGE! I was so re-energized that I cleaned the hall closet and beneath the bathroom sink, and read comfortably until I could fall asleep. *Use this information and you will be dazzled at how much more en-ergy you have to do all those things required of you.*

I urge each of you to do this exercise when you awaken. It will open your spiritual vision/imagination "so you can see where you're headed" on that day. It also gives you clar-ity of thought.

At noon, it takes energy to digest your food. Place your hands over your eyes for a few minutes, and rather than feeling sluggish, you will have the energy you need for the afternoon.

While you're falling asleep at night, place a pillow be-neath one arm to support it, and while you're lying on your side . . . place your hands over your eyes. As you're falling asleep you will review your day, but with your hands in this position, negativity you've unknowingly taken on will dis-solve. If your hands aren't affectionately stroking your pretty lady, or ladies, if your hands aren't on your hunka/ hunka burnin' love . . . place them over your eyes.

An "energy vampire" is one of those people who walks in to your life, sits down, unloads, and—when they depart— they feel uplifted, but you feel hammered. I also suggest, if you're with an energy vampire during the day, which is usu-ally our best friends and family members (and I mean that in the nicest way)—give them the energy, attention, advice, and love they need. But the moment they walk out, rub your hands together and "beef up" your energy field (and get ready for the next one).

I also advise, "When you're sitting on the *throne,* unless you're reading one of my books . . . what better thing do you have to do with your hands? Take every opportunity to keep your energy as high as possible.

If you have unknowingly taken on negativity, or if you smoke, when you place your hands over your eyes, fearful energy is dissolved. You may even lose all desire to smoke or drink or cuss . . . countless habits can be healed with this simple hand position. While you're lying in this position, at night, you may also experience "shifts/electrocutions/heavy sighs/twitches." (Your mate might also.) These body validations will demonstrate that a "shift in consciousness" is occurring.

As a teacher, I always advise NOT to take another's pain deliberately . . . but this is one tip I don't follow myself. Because I am conscious of how to dissolve it, I knowingly take on another's pain "to get it out of them," and I purify it during the night. Most of the aches and pains you now feel aren't even yours. You, through compassion, or empathy, have unknowingly been carrying someone else's discomfort. Lay hands over your eyes. We don't care "whose it is," we just want it dissolved.

Years ago, my mom called and said, "Vicki was just diagnosed with uterine cancer." Just as my mother's voice cracked, she begged, "Oh my God, Gloria, please do something." So I did. I called my sister and talked to her for two hours, consciously "taking on her cancer." The following day, I joined Nikki as she flew to Seattle to speak before five hundred troubled teens about drug abuse. I was hemorrhaging the entire time I was away. (Vicki had been, and now she wasn't.) When she returned to her doctor, she was advised, "You don't have cancer any more." Of course she didn't. I did.

I bled heavily for three days and now I was tired of it. I lay upon the bed and silently said, "Okay God, I know I shouldn't have done this . . . but I did, and now I need a little extra help." A small electric bolt of energy started down at my ankles and continued up my body. The "lightning bolt" of intense energy forced my legs apart, into a "V," and a very sharp electrocution zinged up through my crotch AND I DIDN'T BLEED ANOTHER DROP. The cancer was dissolved.

Again, I'm not asking you to take on another's discomfort consciously. But if you do . . . or if you have unknowingly taken on a loved one's pain, you now know how to dissolve it. In all the years I've done this, I have never carried another person's pain beyond seventy-two hours.

With this valuable information out of the way, now I can offer the message that brings us all together this evening.

At approximately 11:00 P.M. last Sunday night I was extremely tired, and when I burn out to that point, I just want to sit and cry. Childlike, I can get grumpy as well. I've noticed lately anyway that my emotions are on edge and I'm not only highly sympathetic, but also extremely sensitive. I can cry at the drop of a hat, which is due to the rising of my energy and expansion of consciousness. I'm headed toward another new level—I can always feel it as it happens.

Back to my original point. I was tired Sunday night and Kirk made a comment in a tone I didn't care for. However, I said nothing. He went into our home office, and I was grumbling under my breath as I put the china and silverware away from the company meal I'd served. I stepped off my stool and my foot stuck to the floor. Big mistake. I noticed a trail of dirt-over-sticky on the floor around the table, and my mind flashed on my grandson walking around with his so-called spill-free cup.

Grrrr . . . I had just mopped the floor before our guests arrived. I can sometimes be neurotic with my family. Now was one of those times, and it seemed to be enough reason to head to the family office and express my opinion to Kirk over his earlier remark.

As I approached the doorway of the office, however, I saw him behind the computer. Kirk is still the most handsome man I've ever met. From across the room, I looked at him for a moment and my heart melted. I approached him from behind and put my arms around him and slid my hands down the front of his shirt, fluffing his chest hair with my fingers. I bent down and touched my cheek to his, kissed him on the side of the neck, and told him I loved him with my whole, great big heart. I teasingly bit him lightly on the ear and departed from the room with a smile.

Re-entering the kitchen, I grabbed a paper towel and wet it. Re-energized from the love I felt for Kirk, I went around the kitchen, mopping up all the sticky spots Colton's apple juice had made. (As you allow your heart to open, anger and judgments dissolve without human effort.)

The next morning, over coffee before he left for work, I shared my feelings with Kirk from the previous night. I told him of the sensitivity toward his earlier comment, my exhaustion, and final frustration over the dirty floor. I completed my sermonette with the following sentiment, "Kirk, I was empty and tired from all the giving throughout our holiday. But when I saw you sitting in the office, my heart melted. When I hugged you, it refilled me from all the love I feel for you and I was able to go on."

Sincerely, he accepted the compliment and cleared his throat, somewhat embarrassed by the emotion it brought up in him.

I've always been able to express my feelings more easily than most people. I have so dang much love, I have to give it. I tell strangers on the street how pretty they look. But there have been times I didn't express my feelings and felt cheated later.

Two months ago, I was informed of the death of a high school friend. I haven't taken it well. He never knew I was a healer. I didn't know he had cancer of the lungs and was suffering. I've been told I can't be all things to all people—but I want to be as effective as possible so that needless suffering, whether it's one of my friends or one of yours, never needs to occur.

I never had the pleasure of meeting my friend Randy's mother, Rose, until we shared our grieving with each other. I hesitated to tell her I am a healer or to gift her with my books in order to achieve peace in his passing. I meditated for several days, only wanting to do what would be for her highest good. I knew she would feel anger in receiving this knowledge when it was too late. I felt compelled to send her the books.

She was angry and I give her permission. I am angry, too. Divine Order doesn't always make (human) sense. But, from Randy's life and death, we can all learn a lesson through a personalized tale I wrote for Rose. All my tales are written concerning real people, true experiences, and with emotion. I wish I could tell you the stories behind every fairy tale I've been inspired to write. However, I'll be grateful to share the following.

Angels Walk Among Us
(A loving tribute to Randall N. Russell)

Once upon a present-day time, a fair maiden, named Gloria, found herself in deep contemplation of a dear friend from her past. It was just recently that she'd been told of his passing. Though it had been many years since she had seen him, the love for this man had never died. It seemed as if only yesterday they had been together.

Her thoughts returned to yesteryear. It was one score and nine years ago when Gloria's gallant knight called upon his faithful friend, Sir Russell, to watch over her while he was off conquering other lands. As she was walking her path in life, it seemed at first like any other day. When she became aware that life threw her a curve and in confusion she lost her way, she had nowhere to turn. The maiden felt scared and so alone—when Sir Russell and his "Mustang" came to her rescue . . . to safely take her home.

Smiling broadly, he gently held her elbow as he opened her door with loving care, and in that moment, the maiden knew (within her heart of hearts), he was an answer to her prayer.

. . . Returning in thought to present day, Gloria knelt down at her hope chest and slowly turned the key. The trunk held memories of a lifetime. As she raised the heavy lid, the scent of cedar filled her senses.

Lifting an old prom dress from the chest, she smiled and stroked the soft, blue velvet. Sir Russell had taken her to the ballroom dance, at the request of his dear friend, who was unable to return from battle. A deep and heavy sigh filled the maiden's lungs with the forest scent of cedar as her thoughts returned to that evening. Sir Russell complimented her beauty as he danced with her under the stars. She even felt pretty when she saw her reflection in the sparkle of his beautiful eyes.

He was such a gallant gentleman and the dearest friend one could find. She trusted him, believing no harm would ever touch her while in his presence. Memories of him came to mind and she recalled a tune she wrote just for him.

I believe that angels walk among us with God's glorious power,
To lift us above our fears, in what seems our darkest hour.
They show us simply how to live, they teach us how to give,
They come from somewhere, up above, and teach us how to love. . .

Gloria always believed Sir Russell was an angel, cloaked in bodily form. Not that he didn't make mistakes or that he was too pure to be around and be yourself, but because she had never met anyone quite like him. He always made her smile, and whenever she was with him, she believed everything was going to be okay. She felt only pure joy, peace, and security in his presence. He always made her feel special.

. . . Within Gloria's hope chest, hidden in the bottom of her childhood jewelry box, was the small beaded bracelet of a newborn babe. With her tiny middle and index fingers side to side, she slipped the wee bracelet upon them. The baby's bracelet fit perfectly, symbolizing how little Sir

Russell had been, born prematurely. He had grown to six-foot-one.

The string had yellowed from age and she straightened the little blue-and-white-lettered beads to read:

R. R - u - s - s - e - l - l.

She recalled the day he had given this priceless gift to her. As she wore the bracelet upon the fingers of her left hand, she used her right hand to unfold and reread the letter and obituary that had arrived, telling of his passing. "I'm sure you're aware of the death of my beloved son," and tears flowed once again, just as they had ever since she'd received this news from his mother, Rose. In her hands, she held the symbols of Sir Russell's life and death.

No . . . she hadn't been aware . . .

The maiden felt disappointment that their lives had gone in two different directions. Being an eternal optimist, she tried to be thankful that she had known, and been blessed by, his presence. But frustration returned as she recalled that they had spoken only twice in twenty-nine years.

Gloria was deeply saddened that she had never told him of her gratitude for being the first, and one of the only people, who loved her without condition. She never pretended to be anything or anyone other than her true self. Lo and behold, he loved and accepted her anyway. She believed he deserved to know the gratitude, for he had taught her that she was worthy of love. She was angered that she was a gifted healer and that he had needlessly suffered.

She silently thought, "When I felt lost and fearful, and prayed on bended knee, God sent me a friend to gently set me free." More than once, he'd lent comfort, along with a helping hand . . . sometimes just a phone call, to listen and say, "I understand."

"Why couldn't she be there for him?" she wanted to scream. She knew she may never have the answer. "Why . . . when he was at the dark end of the road of his journey in life . . . why, oh why, couldn't she be the one to light his way with a single ray of hope?"

. . . The maiden placed the letter from Rose carefully into the cedar hope chest and thought of closing it as if it were a chapter in her book of life. She wanted to pretend she didn't know. After all, even though they had grown and gone their separate ways, just knowing he was "somewhere out there," gave her security. Knowing he was gone made her feel insecure and frightened. She had lost a very good friend.

This experience had taught her a very good lesson, however. Not one more moment would go by without letting every single soul in her life know how much she loved and appreciated them. Even though it may be embarrassing at times, she would speak her true feelings aloud beginning immediately. She would never waste another moment in life fretting over insignificant trivial events and details. She would become more flexible and less controlling. The maiden would live every moment to the fullest, and she would be angry if others didn't do the same.

Gloria didn't like these feelings of pain, despair, and loss. She wanted to be cowardly, and whether it was her imagination or not, she swore she could hear Sir Russell's sweet and silent guidance. "Be a brave little angel, Gloria." It was as if he had graced her, once again, with mercy in her time of need. Automatically and unconsciously, she began to hum the tune she used to sing to him.

I believe that angels walk among us with God's glorious power,
To lift us above our fears, in what seems our darkest hour.
They show us simply how to live, they teach us how to give,
They come from somewhere, up above, and teach us how to love.

. . . The maiden lifted her senior yearbook from the hope chest and opened it to Sir Russell's photo. *My . . . what a handsome man he was . . .* So much love resurfaced, and she smiled at the memory he left behind in print.

Gloria started to turn to the page, knowing right where

he'd written his message. It had been opened so many times to that place, however, it wouldn't have been difficult to find if her memory had failed her. She remembered, too— after he had signed the book, before he would place it in her hand, he made her promise something. This was most unlike Sir Russell to do. He had never placed a condition upon their friendship. However, he did now. Hearing how important this was to him, in the deep, rich tone of his voiced plea, Gloria knew she would honor the request. It was: "Do not open and read this until I have driven away." Gloria had agreed.

Sir Russell was becoming a man, first receiving a higher education . . . then off to field training, and then out to sea. He had served his friend and Gloria well as her guardian angel. Courageously, he chose to serve his great nation, and the time had come to say goodbye. He was tall, dark, and handsome . . . and she . . . a petite and fair child-woman. She stood on the upper step as they hugged each other. Their hearts joined. Something deep inside Gloria's heart told her she didn't want to release him. She didn't want to ever let him go . . .

As Sir Russell drove away, he stopped and turned to look back at the maiden. He smiled and even in the distance, Gloria knew she was special to this man. (I don't believe she knew, until now, how much she truly loved him, yet she hesitated in sharing her feelings.) He had places to go and things to do. She didn't have the right to interfere with his choices. Besides . . . she'd heard a quote of selfless love, "If you love someone, set him free. If he comes back, it was something meant to be." Smiling softly, she kissed her fingertips and waved goodbye to her best friend.

. . . She opened the yearbook and in his rolling, large handwriting, she read . . . "Gloria, I've always cherished you, and your cute personality has meant a lot to me. I might not have seemed like a real lover, but among all your other admirers, I never had a real chance. But in the future,

I hope the chance will come. I have always thought you were the cutest girl in the kingdom, and you always will be. I only wish that I wasn't leaving or that you were coming along with me. But it wouldn't be fair to disappoint all the other chaps. I will always love you more than you will ever know." He signed it simply . . . Randy.

She hadn't known, until now, how deeply he'd felt toward her. He had been an honorable man to his friend and he had never overstepped his boundaries, being only a gentleman to Gloria.

Sir Russell never came back to her. She saw him again briefly, but she never got the chance to let him know she loved him, too.

Carefully, she placed the yearbook back into the hope chest, knowing that someday her heirs would find these priceless treasures but never know the true value they'd had in their mother's life. No one would ever know unless she put it into written form.

Before she lowered the lid, the maiden's attention fell upon a single, red pressed rose lying quietly in the chest. Another gift of love from Sir Russell. He had given so many . . . He had been the first to ever gift her with a dozen, red, long-stemmed roses. She had dried and pressed one of the roses as a keepsake. As she held the flower in her hand and the memory in her heart, Sir Russell's mom, Rose, came to mind.

Suddenly Gloria understood. Perhaps she hadn't been able to be the spark of hope to her youthful flame, but she could attempt to bring peace to his mother. Randy wouldn't have wanted it any other way. In fact, in remembering the way he spoke of his love for the women in his life, Gloria could only believe it was he who was inspiring this idea. And so she wrote, *"Dearest Rose, I believe that angels walk among us with God's glorious power, to lift us above our fears, in what seems our darkest hour. They show us simply how to live, they teach us how to give, they come from somewhere, up above, and teach us how to love. . . .*

May this gift bring peace to her heart and to yours. Let not another moment pass before I tell you how deeply loved and appreciated you are. Hug/hug/kiss/kiss (and a "peench" on the hiney). Good night, be safe, be happy; I love you with my whole, great big heart.

Gloria, if you wouldn't mind very much, I'd like to skip dinner tonight and have some quiet time in my room at Fred and Dorothy's. My heart is so completely filled, I don't think I could eat a bite. And your speech tonight was everything I needed to hear. In fact, I watched the faces in the crowd, and I noticed that every single eye was on you, and they each hung on your every word. I've been to speakers, around the world, and I've never seen anyone command an audience like you do.

Those people, tonight, walked in with long, sad faces. When you took the stage, I watched as their pain and sadness faded and smiles replaced their heartaches. I know you're not going to accept it as "you" doing anything, because it's just who you are, so I'll compliment you in a way you can easily accept. The Presence of God within does go before you and prepare your way, and luckily for all of us, that little Gloria is important, too. He needs you to work through. I love you so much, Gloria, thank you for this day.

Thank you, but this is embarrassing to me. I know the speech told you to express your loving thoughts, but I'm a reflection of you and others, remember? It's difficult, sometimes, for me to accept too. When the student is ready, the teacher appears. Whenever I'm speaking, I'm to be counted among the students as well.

Give me a hug. If you need me for anything, just holler. Good night, my precious, I love you, too.

Part Three

DON'T TAKE IT
PERSONALLY

22

Guts and Glori(a): From Fear to Eternity

Dr. Glo-bug, it was even hard for me to say good-bye to Fred and Dorothy. While you were showering and packing up this morning, I went downstairs for an early visit with Dorothy as you used to do. She's so beautiful and wise, and Fred let me listen to their daughter's CD of beautiful piano music. I'll have to send her a personal thank-you when I get back home.

After listening to you, I can see that mostly everything you relate in your teachings and individual life revolves around establishing a sense of Oneness in your consciousness, and surrendering judgment. Dorothy, however, mentioned that your sense of peace also comes from "not taking things personally." Could you please share this understanding with me, too?

You're a fast learner. Establishing Oneness with an individual means there is only one body, one mind, one state of consciousness that needs to be risen from human to Divine.

Surrendering judgment of two powers, good and evil, restores your consciousness to God and all creation as spiritual good that has no opposite.

Concerning "not taking it personally," here is the first illustration that comes to mind.

One evening, Kirk came home and said that his employer was closing the mill because of high electric rates. He began to verbally attack the publishing company that we had created to self-publish my books. The company had never grown to a financially successful level to support us. I didn't think self-help books, locked away in a warehouse, could help anyone—so I listened to my heart and gave them freely.

I found myself taking offense during the discussion, as if it were a child of mine who was being berated, scolded, and judged.

I stood in the company's defense, affirming its success. We didn't owe anyone, and had donated countless books to convicts or those who couldn't afford to purchase them. We had already served God and humanity well, even if we never did any more . . . or never showed a profit. We, however, had never paid ourselves. We used the profits to reprint more books to give freely.

Later, following this discussion, I was hoofing it around the neighborhood as I do each night in the rain, snow, or subzero weather. It's my quiet time nightly, away from the constant ringing telephone, a chance to hear my personal messages through the voice of my soul. While walking, I received an "aha" moment of awareness. "Don't take it personally. Kirk is projecting his fears—they aren't yours—understand and accept where he is—be as One and return to love."

Upon my return home, I gave Kirk permission to feel his fears and honor them. He's the breadwinner of the home, responsible to provide for his family. I may know the truth that God is the source and supply, but He also needs Kirk as an avenue of the expression of abundance.

Once Kirk realized I wasn't going to "airy/fairy console or negate the physical reality of providing," he naturally returned to love. Before the evening had ended, he affirmed that he knew we'd be okay . . . we might need to relocate and find new employment, but as One, in harmony, everything would work out. It did. Kirk didn't lose his job.

Karmic law is not a respecter of persons. You don't consciously sit around and try to think of ways to make your life a living hell. Your thoughts flow from a human state of consciousness, which helps you understand why sometimes you feel nervous for no reason or scared. It's "in the air." Fear is a sneaky hummer—return to love, raising your consciousness.

But, Gloria, how do I raise my consciousness? How do I NOT take fear, pain, verbal attack, and so on personally?

Negativity is not yours—don't claim it as yours.

As an example, remember last night's speech? If I awaken and my hip hurts, I don't affirm it as mine because I do not have a body, mind, or soul separate from God. "Someone's hip hurts and I don't have an opinion about it." Instantaneous miracles can happen. EXPECT ONE!

If you wish, I'll continue with some examples. See how many situations occur that we could take personally if we didn't know better . . . and even when we do. My beliefs and presence can threaten and overwhelm people, depending on their fears and beliefs. I accept them where they are and *I don't take it personally.* Also, I'll share some of my previous fears to help make you aware of your potential concerns as you continue to grow.

Yes, please, tell me more. I'm not going to interrupt you; I am just going to lean back and listen and absorb every-

thing you can share. I feel the warmth of the sun coming through the window and the warmth from your heartfelt teachings. Go, girl.

Over the years, it seemed my passion for God was growing, but alas, so were my fears. Readers of *Go Within or Go Without* only had one concerned suggestion, according to the letters I received. They thought the book was too positive and that it was difficult for them to relate some of the material to their lives. They also wished I had given more information concerning the fears I had relating to my spiritual growth, to better identify their individual experiences.

There was no way possible to write everything I would have liked included in that teaching manual, and my continued writings give bits and pieces to the levels we achieve as we open ourselves daily to the Presence of God.

In all truth, I didn't have fears (concerning my healing talent) in the beginning ten years before I went public, other than being concerned that too many people would discover the gift. However, as I persevered to heighten my consciousness, the levels and intensity of which Spirit worked through me changed considerably. Without a teacher "with skin on" to answer my questions and concerns, I found myself uncomfortable when asked to lay hands upon people.

Before I share more information concerning that, I'd like to make myself as "real" as possible, concerning the "real world" we live in, to help you see how I handle events that I felt should be omitted from inspirational writings.

In fifteen years of being a spiritual healer, I've had two obscene phone calls. I guess that's pretty good odds since my name and home phone number were included in more than ten thousand books across the nation. Imagine how you would feel, if, while cooking breakfast one morning, a call comes through and a man says, "I need your help."

With a lilt in your voice, you say, "How may I serve you, Sir?"

"Help me before I rape the baby." (And then he hung up.)

Your heart thuds. Was this a prank call or was it someone who sincerely needed help? You, as a human, can't be the judge or brush the possibility of the reality from your mind . . . so you have your husband finish cooking breakfast and you open yourself to the Light, to be used. Regardless of whether the man was going to actually commit this insane act or if it was "just a prank call," his soul needed to be restored to sanity and wholeness.

Imagine being invited as a guest on a Chicago radio station, with eighteen states listening. You feel blessed that so many people will hear of the possibility to heal their lives. During the interview, however, you realize that not only the interviewer but also his sidekick have actually "set you up" for failure—to mock you and your beliefs—and to do so rudely.

Imagine a radio station that allows the airwaves to deliver disgusting comments to the listeners. Mocking Jesus, saying "He probably pissed in the Nile . . ." was but one of the comments. I spent forty-five minutes on the line, handling myself professionally, with integrity. (While on the phone, I never took any of their comments personally.) Several call-ins were rude and obnoxious as well. I stayed on the line in the event there might be one listener who needed my services. I spent the time with my eyes closed, opening myself to the Presence of God . . . flooding the station with violet Light.

At one point, the host of the show said, "Whewie. Maybe we'd better be careful or lightning will hit the station." I silently thought, "Too late. Your lives are going to change. 'You' invited me to your station." Dirt will rise. I've seen some of these situations in which you feel as if you're drowning in tar as the purification of the soul occurs.

I wrote a letter to the station manager, and out of privacy I'll withhold his name and the name of the station. I'm not sharing this information with you in order to gossip or be rude, I'm sharing one of the down-to-earth negative experiences I've had in connection with my gift.

Once the interview was completed, however, my human side kicked in. I was so angry that day, I could barely see straight. The letter was nowhere near as strong as I wished to make it. Seldom do I feel anger, but I had plenty of human thoughts of how disgusting this entire situation was. All I could do was open myself to be used. I said, "God, I'm really ticked off and I know I should love the host, but there's no way possible for me to do that. Not even a little. But I am willing to no longer take it personally, and I am willing for you to love him through me." I went within and was bathed by the Light. A half an hour later, I felt purified and could probably even meet this man in person and not tae-bo kick him in the head.

Being challenged publicly was one of my fears. I drew it to myself for the experience to become aware of how I would handle myself in that situation. Okay. Now I've learned.

Again. I had lived my spiritual experiences without fear until the power became so intense flowing through me. When I first met "Prince William" I asked his mother, Diana, if he had a cold because his breathing was so stuffy. She replied that he'd been like that since he was born. I held and rocked the baby, giving a bottle, and then burped him. I placed him in his cradle on his back, his eyes immediately opened, and he fidgeted uncomfortably. I turned him onto his tummy and began doing the figure-eight massage, which I teach in the workshops and in *Go Within or Go Without*. (Diana told me later than he'd never been able to rest on his back since he was born.) Following the back massage, he slumbered peacefully for the longest time, his mother shared, since he'd been born.

A day later, he was placed in my arms so she could run and get the vehicle in order to drive me to the airport. She asked if I'd hold her little prince while she retrieved the vehicle, since it was extremely windy. I was pleased to once again hold the child. However, as she placed him in my arms, I could feel the extreme heat of both his lungs as they lay against my right palm.

Immediately, his little eyes rolled back into his head, he smiled sweetly at me, his pulse dropped, and he went limp in my arms. I felt that zzzssstt of adrenaline flow through me and my human thoughts raced wildly as I thought, "Oh God, how embarrassing. When Diana returns to us, I can just say, *Oh sorry, I held your baby* for *only a moment and he died in my arms*." I no sooner thought this terror then Diana re-entered the room. I thrust Prince William into her arms and he awoke.

As she placed him in the car seat and entered the freeway, he began screaming. His five-year-old brother attempted to give him a bottle and Prince William refused. His grandmother, sitting in the back passenger seat of the van, also made a vain attempt. As I was undoing my seat belt to go back to the child, Diana replied, "Oh, you don't need to bother—he can just cry himself to sleep." I begged to differ. I did need to do this. The healing had begun in my arms and he wanted the rest of it.

I sat next to his car seat and rubbed my hands together, intuitively placing my left palm above his head, approximately an inch away from his hair. My right hand went to the front of his lungs. In the palm of my left hand, it felt as though hot lava was flowing out the top of this baby's crown chakra. The heat in his lungs was intense. Within approximately three minutes, the heat stopped flowing out of his crown and the lungs became cool. William smiled sweetly again at me and dropped off to sleep without a further whimper.

I've been asked, "If you're a healer, why does your dad drag oxygen tanks around with a medically diagnosed condition of emphysema?" People often confuse my talent with healing people's boo-boos. I am a spiritual healer, not a psychic healer. I am used to heal people's spirits/souls/consciousness.

I asked my dad a year ago, "Why won't you accept the healing instantaneously?" He said, "Well, kid, it took me a lot of years to get to this level and I just don't believe it can be healed overnight. It will take some time." He didn't limit me, he limited God. His belief that it would take a great deal of time manifests as that reality.

When they arrived recently, I was working on his lungs. I listened to him rattle between his shoulder blades and "felt" his right lung kerthunking with every breath. I had him lie on the bed and lying behind him, I placed hands on his lungs and opened myself to the Presence. I silently said the Truth to the best of my ability and level of awareness. "God is the life, breath, and being of my dad and I ask for a conscious realization of that Truth."

I felt three zzzsssts of powerful surging electricity and as before, I felt fear, immediately trying to remove my hands from his lungs. My hands, however, were "super glued" to his lungs and with all my might, I couldn't pull away as I had done with other people. I thought I had killed my dad. I heard no more rattle. There was no more kerthunking of his right lung. My inner fears were making me not want to do healings any more.

I think God is a pretty smart hummer, though. Who better than my own father to teach me what was occurring? As the personality Gloria, I wanted to leap from the bed and run to the kitchen and apologize to Mom. "I'm sorry. Dad's dead. Call 9 1 1."

My dad was still breathing and my heart was pounding from the adrenaline rush. For fourteen years the loving energy flowed. Now it was liquid fire, flowing like a river through me.

Following that healing, Kirk called and asked Dad to join him and two coworkers to go crystal mining. When they returned late that evening, Dad said he was having difficulty breathing. They'd driven to a seven thousand-foot elevation and had done a lot of walking. Kirk teasingly said, "No kidding, Allen. There were times that the others and myself were thinking of knocking you to the ground and taking your oxygen from you, because it was hard for all of us to breathe."

The following morning, Mom said, "You're not going to believe what happened last night. Dad never turned his oxygen on, from the time they left until they returned. He did all that walking at high elevation on his own."

Again that afternoon I was working on dad while he slept comfortably. This time I didn't feel the zzzsssts—now both my hands became pure electricity. I was getting tired of these adrenaline rushes and fears. Although his breathing silenced again, I realized God was still breathing through him. I couldn't go through life, even as an instrument, scaring myself to death every time I opened myself to be used.

I had asked everyone I knew what was happening to me. They all had opinions. Now it was time to ask Jesus.

My inner vision opened and I asked what was happening in my world, and he replied, "You know how I was used as a Mediator in October of 1985 to bring you to the level of Oneness?" I said, "Yes." He continued, "You are now becoming a Mediator to bring others to that same level."

Any time I'd ever seen or talked to Him before, He was

always standing and I could never see a full view of His face. On this occasion, though, He sat in the gazebo and I stood—He and I were now about eye-to-eye, and I, for the first time in fourteen years, noticed how utterly beautiful He was. He smiled a full smile at me and said, "Stay focused, Gloria."

It took almost two decades for me to come to the full realization of the immensity of the gift that's been bestowed upon my soul's life and experience. Puts everything back into perspective, wouldn't you say? Extending the time on a tombstone versus giving others the gift to know God, Direct, hmmm . . . let me see which is of greater importance.

It was worth every fear I felt as the adrenaline rushes transformed into electrical zzzsssts, to the ever-present glowing warmth that "just turns on" as needed. My greatest transformation occurred from being the world's largest "Chicken McNugget" to a gutsy little hummer, attaining the Master State of Consciousness.

Oh my goodness, Gloria, I have so many questions, it would take days for you to answer them for me since I've now heard all this. So many times I've taken things personally . . . not understanding that I didn't need to—or the results—if I'd just allow the situations to be healed. I'll just have "to stay tuned for the continuing books, your chat line on the Web site, and public appearances so that I can learn everything you have to share."

That, my friend, may take all of us throughout eternity to do. . . .

23

A Vehicle of Expression

Glo-bug, just to make this "don't take it personally" tip very solid in my awareness, can you offer one more story? As I said, I believe it's the stories that you tell that will help me and others remember these spiritual principles when we meet some of life's challenges.

At one point in my attempts to get published, a publishing giant was reviewing me. They had my manuscript for a few weeks, when I received a call from a Portland, Oregon, radio station wanting to interview me. During the conversation, the deejay realized that this publisher was considering one of my books.

Strongly, he said, "Be careful concerning this publisher, Gloria, they are sharks." Like an innocent child, I didn't know what he was referring to and asked him to explain. Again, he barked, "Be careful. I said they're sharks."

I was beginning to feel fear, but I still didn't understand what that meant. Not realizing my innocence, he replied, "Maybe I was never supposed to interview you. Maybe God is using me as your guardian angel today, just to forewarn you about this publisher."

As I hung up the phone, I made my way to the "love seat" in the living room. I was reviewing the deejay's words over and over in my mind when I thought, "Ha. I'll just be a shark's enemy." I continued to ponder, however, "What *is* a shark's enemy?" Not having a deep understanding of ocean life, I didn't know what a shark's opponent was.

Immediately I realized, This isn't my nature to try and be an enemy to anyone or anything. Instead, I'll be One with the shark. I'll be the ocean it swims in, the food that sustains its life, and the air it breathes. After all, an author, to a publisher, is what gives them the ability to sustain their business . . .

I wasn't in opposition with the publisher (or a shark, or anything). The forewarning coming from the man's fears was dissolved in love. I was at peace. (The publisher, however, was one more that rejected me.)

As I write my books or speak publicly, I continue to make myself "as real" as I can be for you. I want to create a trust within you that, to the best of my ability, I'm telling you the truth from my perspective.

We are all vehicles of expression for the Divine. God's nature is goodness. He doesn't have the ability to "get even," reign terror in your life, thrust illness upon you, punish, or reward you. God is just God. Goodness. Divine Intelligence. Infinite love, compassion, righteousness, honesty, and so on. We, as humans, have a moment-to-moment ability to choose love or to choose fear. We have the free will to choose to act out dramas in the human experience. We have the right to choose to correct those things which once went wrong. And remember, we can choose to be right or to be happy.

The following is an experience in which, in the end, I chose happiness and doing what my heart said to, it being the right thing to do.

My son D.W. needed to purchase a dependable vehicle. I gasped when he said he'd picked out a new $17,000 vehicle. With his current wages, he couldn't afford it. I persuaded him to buy a used vehicle that was dependable and to save his extra money toward purchasing the newer vehicle he actually wanted. I had hoped to instill patience and perseverance, rather than the commonly expected instant gratification.

When we arrived at the used car company, I asked the salesman, "If you were this boy's father—what car would you recommend as being reliable and affordable?" He agreed upon the same one my son had chosen, a nine-year-old, used Buick Regal Gran Sport.

D.W. had paid his previous vehicle's two-year bank note for his pickup in full within five months. Of course, he had established good credit and easily got the loan for this used car. He drove it for fifteen days and the transmission failed. I called the dealership and asked, "As a demonstration of good will, would you be willing to pay at least half of the car's repair?" They replied, "No. You signed an 'As Is Agreement' and we're not willing to help."

I was angry. I telephoned the bank and explained that D.W. hadn't even made his first car payment. The insurance company said it wasn't covered under his policy unless it was due to an accident. (I teasingly said, "But, it was an accident that we bought the car.) I had the V.I.N. number run by our local police and telephoned the previous buyer. She said the car had transmission problems prior to our purchasing it.

I telephoned my way up the line, to Consumer Affairs, and placed a formal complaint. By state law, no deceit or fraud had taken place. I was told that "this is just what used car companies did."

I spent two months attempting to resolve the problem. My son had driven his car fifteen days and the repairman had it in the shop for twenty-five. The cost for repair escalated from a quoted $800 to $1,450. Not only was the transmission a problem, but the radiator, hoses, and wheel bearings were shot, too.

I had felt so inspired that this car was the one for my son. I felt guilty that the money he had saved to begin life, following graduation, would be spent in this manner.

I awakened early one morning, so angry I could barely see straight. I thought of placing an ad in the local newspaper and asking anyone who had been deceived by the used car company to join me with signs along the highway in front of this man's business. "Buy from someone who has integrity—KEEP GOING." My mind raced with how to destroy this business through word of mouth.

In the silence, I asked myself, "If I were to add this story to one of the next inspirational books I write—what message would I want to share?" My intuition told me, "To wish him success." Yikes. *Who would have EVER thought of that?*

It was time to stop thinking about what my head had to say. I have an extremely high energy level, but did I want to use it toward being constructive or destructive? It was time to stop trying to figure out if I should get an attorney or call senators, congressmen, or walk and talk my way up through the White House. It was time to listen to my heart. I have a memory like an elephant, so I'll quote you what I wrote.

Dear Sir:

I want you and your family's company to be successful. I would like you to know the warmth and caring of this community that I have felt in the ten years of living in Stevensville.

The second time I went into Bi-Lo (our local grocery store), I asked a cashier where I could find a certain item and she replied, "You'll find it on aisle number 7, Gloria." I stopped and looked at her in awe, that she knew my name. I had lived in Sacramento, California, for ten years, and I had to show my I.D. at the same grocery store the entire time I lived there.

I want Stevensville to open their arms to you and help you become prosperous and trusted, and for you to know the acceptance a small town has to offer.

You and I have started off our acquaintance on the wrong foot. I would like to extend my hand and introduce myself. I am a housewife, mother (to four kids), an inspirational author and speaker, a spiritual teacher, minister, doctor of religious studies, and a published songwriter. My New York publisher is bringing my first (of four) into bookstores nationwide in August of this year. They have hopes of making me the spiritual Erma Bombeck of the twenty-first century.

My writings teach how to blend spirituality into every moment of your life.

As I awoke this morning, I felt angry over the recent experience with your company. I, of course, like everyone, have an ego—and my mind raced with ways to publicly destroy any future business for you. But as a spiritual teacher—trying to walk my talk and teach my readers how to handle everyday occurrences of conflict—I had to ask myself, "What would be the message of this experience that I would want to share?"

The answer is the first sentence I wrote on your letter today. If I look at you, as an aspect of me—and what I would want for myself, I could only ask that you be successful and accepted in this community.

I apologize, too, that I took any of this experience personally concerning the used car we purchased from you. Unfortunately, used car dealers and salesmen have been criticized, condemned, and judged. You do offer affordably priced vehicles to those who can't afford a new one. (My mother bought a new Ford and the transmission failed . . . she had no warranty coverage.)

I write books and have forthcoming media coverage across the nation, and my goal is to make a difference in this world. I can only achieve that if I walk my talk and demonstrate peace and love in my individual life.

Before my son bought the Buick Regal, I prayed and asked to be guided to the right car for him. The next morning, "I knew" the Regal was the car for him. On our drive to your used car lot, I noticed a rainbow above your company. I took that as a sign, confirming our choice.

Imagine my confusion, then, as the situation unfolded. I continued to wonder why I had been attracted to this experience. What was I getting out of it? Of course, now I know. I had one more opportunity to remove fear and anger and return to love.

Again, I don't want to see you fail in the business you have chosen that supports your family or serves the people in the Bitterroot Valley. I want to help empower you to be the best used car dealership in the nation. To be honest, I don't know how to do that—except to extend a hand of kindness and to show you love, if even in a letter.

I forgive you the debt (of my expectation that you owe my son), in paying half or all of the $1,450 he paid for repair work. (By the way, it wasn't just the transmission; it involved the radiator, hoses, and wheel bearings. I believe the repairman went through the car with a fine-tooth comb, and my son now drives a dependable vehicle.)

I also ask you to forgive me for challenging you or your family's integrity. I am so sorry. I am sending a copy of this letter to those listed below. I hope that it will clear your name and allow me to publicly apologize.

Thank you for your time. I want you and your family to know that this apology is sincere and I'm so sorry for any inconvenience I have caused you.

Always,
Gloria D. Benish

My son wasn't a "victim." Being a part of the mass consciousness, under karmic law of good and bad, means that bad things happen to good people. It is each individual's responsibility to review his or her own beliefs and to transcend karmic law. Everyone creates their reality based upon their loves, hates, and fears. When individuals have a private healing through me, I am able to raise their consciousness from human to Divine, altering their experience. However, unless they continue to incorporate the knowledge on a daily basis, they will not have lasting results.

Countless people become "workshop junkies" or call "for a Gloria fix" when their human experience isn't mirroring what they experienced while sitting in my audience or healing chair. This becomes frustrating to me because I can't be all things to all people. Even Jesus said, "I have to go away or your comforter won't come." The masses came to Him to feed and clothe them, to perform miracles and inspire them. He said, "Ye too can perform the greater works." The people wanted Him to do it for them.

When we open ourselves to the Presence of God, "It" goes before us and prepares our way and day. "It" guides and performs the greater works.

Every day gives each of us an opportunity to be a vehicle of expression for love or fear.

If you lose something physical, you've lost nothing.
If you lose your health, you've lost something.
If you lose your peace of mind, you've lost everything.

My peace of mind is worth far more than $1,450. Peace of mind is priceless . . .

24

Between Saint and Sinner

Oh, Gloria, we're nearing your home and I don't want you to stop talking and being a Voice to those of us who are seeking. I hope we have time for a few more stories. I just can't get enough of them.

I can't believe I've even talked so much this weekend and haven't yet, one time, really talked about one of the highlights of what I do. The nonprofit corporation I founded, Miracle Healing Ministry, was created to help charitable situations, and one of the sidelines of it was the prison ministry program. To date, no donations have gone to administrative costs. All money is used to better the lives of others.

Because of meeting Nikki while she was behind bars, I became quite interested in working with convicts. Our meeting was a validation from Spirit from my earlier years, for I was told one afternoon that I'd be working with convicts and writing books about miracles.

Because I was such a "goody two shoes," I couldn't figure out how that would ever occur. Nikki's and my worlds col-

lided on May 29, 1990, and we began corresponding immediately, using our actual letters to write a book titled
Between Saint and Sinner. It hasn't yet gone to press, but I
hope one day to see it in print or movie form. It has a
"twist" to it, since humanity thinks it's always the saint who
saves the sinner's soul.

One of the most powerful things I ever heard Nikki say
while we were teaching workshops across the nation was,
"Everyone turns to Gloria for help. It took her finding an
ex-heroine junkie, in prison, to find someone to listen to
her." She's an awesome woman. And a great spiritual
teacher . . .

The highlights of my service to mankind "is getting to go
to prison" and having the opportunity to teach inmates
how to heal their lives. Convicts can't go to a self-help
bookstore or call in a reliable therapist, so the money I receive for teaching workshops has provided the ability to
send books into the prisons and into the actual hands of
those they can help. All donations made from private healings allow the ministry to buy other inspirational/self-help
authors' writings to place them into the hands of men and
women who can find peace, hope, and love.

On my last trip into the Chowchilla State Women's
Prison in Chowchilla, California, Robert Peck, substance
abuse class counselor, told me that I would be allowed to
teach three consecutive workshops, consisting of 210
women. He and the other teachers involved would be
cramming as many inmates into a classroom as possible. I
only had one fear. Being third-generation motormouth and
limited to two hours for each session—would I have
enough time to teach as much as I wanted them to learn?

The first class went exceptionally well, I thought. I had a
couple of skeptics in the crowd, but I always love skeptics.

No one was going out of her way to be rude, just inquisitive. With the second class, however, came frustration. Small pockets of women in this group were whispering and talking the entire time. It was almost an hour into the class and I hadn't yet received their attention. As the whispering continued, I was beginning to take it personally.

When I finished teaching, the women rushed to the front of the room for hugs and quickly started asking questions *in Spanish.* I didn't know, until I was finished, that I was speaking before a Spanish class, and those who were talking while I was . . . were translators! (I just rolled my eyes, because I feel as silly repeating this as I did when it happened.) A gentle reminder for you and me: Remember, we don't always see the "whole plan" nor have all the facts as we are making human judgments about situations. Don't take other people's opinions/judgments personally. Nor your own.

The third class was the largest group of women. I gave as many hugs as each asked for. These women are hungry for love and there's no touching or hugging allowed behind prison walls. I wasn't going to say, "You've already had a hug—no more for you." If they wanted four, they got four.

At the end of my talk, a tall woman approached me and asked for a hug. She had a "ho hum—don't really want one—but everyone else is" attitude at first. She held me casually in her arms, but then tightened her hold. She projected telepathically that she felt as if she was hugging Christ and she'd forgotten how good it felt.

I telepathically heard a second thought that she wanted to pull me completely into her heart center. If I had been claustrophobic I would have been in trouble, because by now she had me tucked in her armpit and was pulling me even closer.

I thought about being afraid, but figured if someone saw my eyes bugging out from being squeezed so hard, they would step in to stop her.

When I complete any healing, I always say, "Give me a hug and don't let go until I tell ya." I do this because while we're hugging, I'm "scanning" and making sure I have every energy block dissolved. I'm purifying the recipient's bloodstream and every major organ as I gently run my hand up and down his or her spine. I'm balancing their entire energy field.

Ha. And you thought I was just a kissy/huggy kind of gal. Nope. I'm working up until the last second of contact.

Because I didn't stop this woman from being within my energy field and being in control of how much energy she'd be drawing from me, as we parted from the hug, she began shaking. Her hands were quivering with energy and she became frightened.

She stood back, looking at me with questioning eyes, not quite understanding what was occurring. She repeated, "Oh my God. Oh my God." Each time with greater and louder intensity, which attracted the attention of everyone in the room. I waited until she had captivated all the attention before I began to speak. "Now you know how it feels to be in my skin all the time with that much energy—and now you know why I'm so grateful to freely give it away."

To my right, I intuitively knew a woman's abdomen was hurting, and I guided the power-packed inmate to the woman in need, to offer a helping hand. Within minutes of her laying hands on, the energy was bled into the woman and the pain immediately dissolved. The overly stimulated convict was back in balance, as well. Ta da! Don't you just love it when instantaneous miracles occur and everyone realizes they can do this, too?

Mr. Peck had written my publishing and ministry's name and address on the bulletin board of each classroom, sharing with the inmates that I send free books to anyone who writes requesting them. Days after I arrived home, I had a mailbox full of requests for free books. Each inmate wrote a letter, requesting the answers to questions, as well as autographed books. I sat in my living room for eighteen hours straight fulfilling these requests. The following morning, I devoted six more hours and drove to the post office. I backed in and got a cart to carry the books into the building and spent $94 in postage to mail them.

Each time I went to the mailbox, I was swarmed with more and more requests as word-of-mouth discussions continued.

I had been told that I'd be allowed to go to the prison's TV studio and record my teaching the inmates, thereby giving them a future tool to continue to teach more convicts.

From that trip into Chowchilla Prison, I'm sharing a letter, and a portion of another (for privacy):

Dear Gloria,

My name is Judi J. and I am an inmate at C.C.W.F. in Chowchilla, California. I had the privilege of hearing you speak on this past Friday. It is not a day I will soon forget. I wanted to tell you that I have always believed in miracles, but have never experienced one firsthand, until now.

Let me explain: When I came to hear you speak on Friday, I was experiencing the first day of a herpes outbreak. I do not know what you know of this virus, but it starts with a maddening itch, then a boil appears, then you get a few days of that—it "dries" up and a scab forms. When it falls off, you're fine again for another month.

I hope this is not too graphic of a description for you. I do not mean to offend you in any way. I just want to emphasize the importance of my experience in meeting you and experiencing my own personal miracle. As I said, that day was day one. I had a personal contact with you via a "hug." Also, I was first in the (what I refer to as) your "circle of love." I was the short blonde (well, okay, half blonde)—do you remember me?

At any rate, the itching stopped almost immediately and I was afraid to go back to my cell to check the matter out for fear the boil would still be there. Then I remembered what you said about sometimes needing to wait seventy-two hours before the miracle manifests itself. I felt no symptoms that evening. When I awoke the next morning, the boil was totally gone—no scab—no weeklong process—nothing. I got down on my knees and thanked God and thanked Him for sending you to me.

I do not believe in coincidence. I believe there was a reason I was there that day. I believe the reason was to meet you and help you pass on Jesus' word of love for one another. Thank you for being you—you do, indeed, have a "great big heart."

Needless to say, I am very interested in the notion of receiving the book you mentioned, *Go Within or Go Without*. I believe I can help spread the word and I believe I, too, can learn what you have to teach. I have been trying the method you outlined to us, but have not yet been able to see the "violet Light." I will keep on trying until I do achieve this.

Could you please send me a copy of your book? I will greatly appreciate any further help you can give me with this matter. I hope to hear from you soon.

Sincerely,
Judi J.

P.S. Thank you from the bottom of my great big heart.

A second letter that arrived in the same stack of mail comes from a woman with the initials T.C. She begins:

It was an honor and privilege to have met you at C.C.W.F. in Chowchilla. Of the many people you met that day, I was not one of the skeptics. As a matter of fact, I sat through your first and second sessions that day. I wish I could've sat through the third session, but I didn't want to be greedy. I figured that was a seat that another could use, and so I went about the rest of my day and continued business as usual.

T.C. went on to say that her *real* mother was also present that day. Throughout this lengthy letter, she was asking for a miracle for her mother and other close family members. It's letters like T.C.'s that inspire me to continue my ministering to those behind bars.

I'm convicted of killing my stepfather, who was an abuser. The crime took place at the end of 1988 and I've been locked up since 1989. I have a twenty-five-to-life sentence, but so does my mom. You see, she has no alibi and the jury, confused as they were, couldn't decide whether she was guilty or not. They clearly stated they did not know who did the crime. So, with the Rodney King riots going on, these folks wanted to get home, too. In the end, a confused and undecided jury convicted both of us and went home. My mom did not commit the crime. I did. The jury just didn't pay attention.

Anyhow, I reckon I won't be going anywhere real soon. Problem is, neither will my mom. And while I protected her from her abuser, I cannot protect her from glaucoma. I can't protect her from all life's ills, aches, and pains. I just want her to leave this place alive one day. Alive, healthy, and whole.

T.C.'s letter went on to explain that once they were sentenced, she was scared, but the reality of her actions and sentencing hadn't sunk in. Once it did, she grew angry and very bitter. Not with herself handling it all wrong, but with God. She blamed the whole circumstance on God. She stopped praying and condemned Him for the hell He had made as her home. To get even, she turned to Satanism. She felt powerful, hateful, and evil. A friend, however, started planting seeds in T.C.'s mind, and they argued their beliefs.

One evening as she sat on her bed in the dark, she was looking out the window at a black sky. She said these words, "God, there's a spiritual war taking place inside me. I'm confused. I'm lost. If you really want my soul, my love, I need a sign. I don't need a full-fledged miracle, but just a sign that cannot be mistaken for anything else, but from you. If you can forgive me for turning my back on you, I need to know. I need to know if *you* really want *me*."

The very next day, she got her miracle. A Bible mysteriously appeared on a stack of clothing. She opened it at random and an inner voice spoke, "You've gone too far." She turned more pages, closer to the front. "You've still gone too far." She turned closer to the front and in the Gospel of John, she read, *He who walks in darkness does not see where he is going.*

T.C. wept. As she cried tears of regret, sorrow, and remorse, her soul was healed and her life transformed.

Since that day, Spirit has used T.C. to reach out to troubled youths, and she is now chairperson of a "U-Turn Drug Prevention Program." She works and counsels one-on-one with kids who have been in abusive situations. She's an awesome woman. She's helped 580 women, and approximately 1,000 kids a year for the past three years. She's found her purpose for being where she is. Good or bad, who's to say? Some of God's greatest servants are behind bars, because He sends each of us where we need to be.

As I was walking out of the classroom that day, with a

"body of women taking each step with me," another lifer walked up to me for a final hug. As we held each other, she whispered, "Society hates us, Gloria. Thank you for loving us in spite of our mistakes." (Kinda gets ya, doesn't it?) And people ask me, "If you don't charge, Gloria—what do you get out of all this?"

I wonder. . . .

25

World Peace Begins
With(in) Me

Gloria, others and myself can admire the peace you feel and experience. Everyone in the world would like to know peace, and with your teachings, I can now see how I can help the bigger picture by incorporating your life-saving tips. We're just a few miles from your "home" . . . and since you're aware of my "personal loss," could I have you please just give me a little more understanding about the death process? Also, I feel as if we've become such good friends, could you relate a story of another who "just dropped into your life" unexpectedly and the results of that meeting?

In 1995, when I went public with my healing gift and desire to teach others how to heal their lives, our local newspaper interviewed me. The interviewer spent nearly two hours with me, asking questions, and I offered examples concerning each one. She was beautiful and pleasant and, I believed, truly interested.

Imagine my surprise as I was walking her to the door

and giving her a heart-to-heart hug, she responded skeptically, "Ya, know, I just don't know if I believe any of this."

I was shocked. She had seemed so open-minded. I took her attitude personally and felt offended, fearing the type of article she could write. I've seen other healers or gifted people chastised by the public and with my first foot "coming out of the closet," I didn't want to deal with adversity.

I responded, "Up until now, I've only been known as the lady who wears bells on my shoes, a smile on my face, and a kind word for everyone I meet." With great authority I said, "And just because you found out I can do all this, I'd better *never* be treated any differently in this town."

As I closed the door, I looked to the ceiling, surrendering my fear and said, "God, I'm a little busy to be worrying about this—*You write the article.*"

Twice a year, complimentary copies of this newspaper are sent out to everyone in the Bitterroot Valley. The edition with my article happened to be one of those gifted copies. When I read it, you would have thought my best friend had written it.

I received countless requests for spiritual guidance, healings, and "atta boy's for going public with the information." Two friendships began, due to that article.

Days after the article came into print, I received a call from Michelle. She asked whether she could come by to meet me and, of course, I welcomed the opportunity to get to know her. Sitting at my kitchen table and having lunch with me, she said she'd read the newspaper and that evening she had a dream where I told her "Michelle, step into the Light." She awoke, not knowing what the message meant.

A second dream in the same night offered the same message. Michelle didn't know what the "Light" meant. As we continued to talk, and I began to teach about the violet Light and It being the healing state of consciousness, she gasped. She saw the violet Light whenever she closed her eyes, but didn't know what it was. Michelle had been unaware she was a gifted healer until we met.

Her husband, Michael, was a skeptic. He wasn't spiritual or religious. When he was a young man, he was caught sleeping with the daughter of a church elder. Michael also was in trouble with the church for smoking marijuana. He was brought before a group of the elders and asked to promise he would never do these things again, being informed the church could forgive him for his past actions.

As a strong-willed teenager with a smart-aleck attitude, he said, "Well, I liked sleeping with your daughter and I like to smoke marijuana, so if I'm honest . . . I don't plan on giving either one of them up." The men left the room and returned with their findings. "God has asked us to have you ex-communicated from this church."

Michael, of course, was angry and decided to rob the elder's home . . . but he was caught and imprisoned.

Religion had left a sour taste in Michael's mouth. Michelle met Michael and did for him what I did for Nikki while she was in prison. She accepted collect phone calls, got quarterly gift boxes together, wrote constantly, visited, and gave undying, unconditional support. When Michael was paroled, they married.

From California they'd moved to Montana, and now Michelle found herself becoming my friend while being married to a nonbeliever, an angry and frustrated skeptic who was getting tired of hearing "Gloria this and Gloria that."

One afternoon I received a call from the overly-Gloria-saturated husband. He told me of his younger years and the ex-communication from his church. Michael said, "I figured if God didn't want me any more—I had nothing else to lose."

He also remarked, "I'm sick of hearing Michelle talk about you. We quarreled the other night and I asked her, 'Do you mean to tell me, if Gloria asked you to jump off a cliff, you'd do it?' and Michelle responded, 'Yes. But you don't know Gloria. She'd never ask me to do that.' "

During our conversation, I gave Michael permission to be angry at the church for their decision. Frightened men in judgment, not God, made that choice. He asked if he could come by to meet me face to face, and I agreed.

Upon his arrival, I asked if he'd like to "feel the experience of what God truly Is," and he resisted, at first. As we continued to talk and he realized I'm just me, that I have no hidden agenda and spoke only from my heart, he agreed to sit in my healing chair.

I closed the drapes and put on my favorite healing music, "Kitaro: Light of the Spirit." I have used the same cassette for fifteen years and it's never worn out, even though I've replayed it over and over for sometimes 12 to 14 hours a day. The healing Light must "regenerate it," because it's as new as it was the day it was given to me. Also, I use Kitaro because more than any other music I've heard, it has the ability to raise a person's consciousness very quickly.

When I finished the "overhaul" on Michael and he'd personally felt the Presence of God, he said, "Gloria, now I understand. If you asked me to jump off a cliff, I would." I giggled and said, "Michael, I'd never ask anyone to do anything that I wouldn't be willing to do myself."

I guess, in their own way, Michelle and Michael were complimenting me, but I would never want nor accept that kind of responsibility. I do not tell people what to do in financial, physical, or health matters. I will teach you all I know to open yourself to the Presence of God within you and allow that Source to be your guide.

The second friendship that came from the newspaper article was with a retired couple, Joe and Pat. Joe called the evening the newspaper came out and asked, "Gloria, can you really do what this paper says you can?" Confidently and sincerely, I replied, "Yes."

That afternoon, Joe's wife, Pat, had been diagnosed with an incurable lung disease. When they returned from the doctor, they were greeted with my bright and smiling face in the article. We scheduled an appointment the following day.

I think Pat came to me for actual healing three or four times. What a beautiful couple they were. Joe was tall and ruggedly handsome with his boots and cowboy hat. His bride, Pat, was the picture of "the perfect grandma we'd all like to have in our life."

After I worked with Pat, she and Joe purchased a new pickup, and a fifth-wheel camper and spent the next three years touring and visiting children and grandchildren, enjoying their golden years together.

In the fourth year of our friendship, I got a call from their daughter, Nancy (from Los Angeles), who was at the St. Patrick's Hospital in Missoula, Montana, about twenty-four minutes from where I live.

"Mom wants to die tonight and she has asked me to call you, to come and take her through the death ceremony." I went totally into fear. *I didn't know how to do that.*

Lovingly I said, "Nancy, my friend Nikki is arriving tomorrow and she's done this three times. I'll pick her up at the airport and bring her straight to the hospital to do this for you and your mom."

Softly, Nancy replied, "That's very kind of you, Gloria,

but my mom doesn't want Nikki—she wants you. And, she doesn't want to die tomorrow, she wants to die tonight."

I started babbling. "I'm in my footie jammers and I'll need to get redressed. . . ." I was giving her far more information than I'm sure she cared to hear, but I do remember committing to the request. I'm a minister, for God's sake. But this was going to be my first time to have an up-close and personal experience with the dying.

Kirk was concerned about me doing this. I had become very emotionally attached to Pat and Joe. They could have been my parents. They wouldn't move from the Bitterroot Valley as long as I lived here, because they knew they were in good hands. I would have found it hard to move far away from them, as well, because of the constant support and love I felt while in their presence.

On the drive into Missoula, I was talking (big time!) to God. "Ya know, God, you're going to have to guide me through every single step and word." I had only my personal experience to relate to, as well as a few dreams and visions.

Before I arrived at the hospital, Pat and Nancy had made a deal. When Pat chose to have the oxygen mask removed, she would squeeze her daughter's hand. Pat had also received a shot of morphine.

As I stepped into Pat's room, you would have thought I was going to a birthday party rather than a "death-day" party. I, of course, wasn't aware how to take anyone "through the ceremony of death" as Nancy had termed it. I did know how to be loving, I can easily hear the inner Voice of my soul, and I can follow instructions quite well . . . especially when I'm scared to death (oops . . . no pun intended).

My bells jingled across the quiet room to Pat's side and

she smiled, her heart warming to know I'd arrived. I was softly stroking her face and excitedly saying, "Pat, the only thing I can tell you to start with is that I've never done anything like this before in my life. What I do know though is, during this process—if you can feel it—I promise it's not going to hurt." I continued, "Since they gave you morphine, you may not feel anything, but since I'm One with you . . . I'll be able to tell you every single thing that's happening, as it occurs."

Still stroking the top of her head and softly touching her face, neck, arms, and hand, I said, "Pat, I know right now you are in a very confused state of mind . . . one foot in the physical world and one foot in the spiritual world. But, in just a few minutes, you're going to become all-knowing of every single thing going on simultaneously in the universe. You're going to know why it's your daughter, Nancy, your son, Eric, standing here at your deathbed . . . and me. You'll know why you married Joe, why you had five children, and why you lost one of them early in life . . . you're going to have every single answer you've ever wanted.

"And since I can't keep a secret—I have to tell you this, rather than waiting for you to get there and find it out. *You're going to find out you never made a mistake in your life. Every single thing you did, you had to do.*"

Still stroking her and telling her that after she crossed over, she would go through a seventy-two-hour (earth time) review of her life. Not until she completed that would I be able "to see or hear her" in dreams or visions.

"In the dimension you'll be living, Pat, no physical words are spoken—all communication will be performed telepathically. So, let's practice. You think a thought and I'll answer. Then I'll think a thought, and you can guide me with your mind."

Pat telepathically asked me to place my left hand atop

her head and my right hand on her heart center, in the middle, above both breasts. I did and she knew immediately I really could hear her thoughts.

In the middle of her back, I felt a tremendous amount of electricity gather. She stiffened with fear. She knew what this would mean, as did I. Immediately she was filled with adrenaline, which just about fried me as it filled my entire being.

Softly, to lessen her fear, I whispered, "Pat, what you just felt . . . the adrenaline . . . is the Presence of God. You don't need to be frightened, it's okay."

It wasn't just the adrenaline that frightened Pat; it was the huge amount of electricity that had gathered in the middle of her spine. It was the energy that had provided life to the various nerve endings and vital organs. She knew if she relaxed, it wouldn't provide her body with the life force and she was scared.

Softly again, I said, "Pat, please don't be afraid. If you can feel what's going on . . . I promise, as you relax, it won't hurt." She trusted and did relax.

As she did, all the electricity in her body rose to the upper chest where she had asked me to place my right hand. Beneath the palm, it felt like a multitude of pinpricks, such as the feeling when your hand goes to sleep. All the energy of her body was beneath my palm and she telepathically projected, "I'm giving you the rest of my life force . . . to use for yourself . . . or to give to others."

Tears started to stream down my face. I had gone to her death-day party and I was the one who was given the gift. HER LIFE. I'm teary now as I speak these words, remembering that moment.

It felt as if my hand had become a sponge as I absorbed her life's energy. Just as that happened, she squeezed Nancy's hand.

"Oh my God, Mom, are you sure? You want me to re-move the oxygen mask?" Pat squeezed a second time and her daughter removed the mask.

Pat took a deep breath and exhaled. All was quiet in the room as Nancy's voice cracked, asking, "Gloria, did my mom just die?"

"No. In fact, she just telepathically asked me to go to the foot of the bed and stroke from her knees, down her legs, and softly touch her feet."

I did, and a moment later Pat took another breath, ex-haled . . . and IMMEDIATELY was standing to my left. I could see her in my peripheral vision. I said, "Nancy and Eric, your mom is standing here at my side and she has just died with as much grace as she lived. She's asked me to say these words. "All is done now, except those things which are of a necessity. All will be well . . ."

Pat didn't "float" or "walk"—she "thought herself to Nancy's side," placed her arm around her daughter's shoul-der, then she disappeared from my vision.

I couldn't keep my hands off Pat. I continued to stroke her legs and feet, and I was so grateful she had given me this experience to share with others. In that moment, I thought of never attempting to heal another person—but to go into hospice work, because NO ONE SHOULD EVER DIE ALONE, and definitely, **NO ONE SHOULD EVER BE AFRAID OF IT.**

In the closing of my workshops, I tell this as my final miracle story. All that I teach in writings and in person is for your awareness of how to open yourself to the Presence of God and allow "It" to live in and through you. You al-ready are loving, kind, caring, sharing, compassionate, honest, moral, and genuine. Embodied within you is *every attribute that God is.* All That God Is . . . You Are. It's not anything you have to develop, you merely need to be re-minded that you are "already It."

With all my writings and all I've shared, and especially this story, I hope you will understand that as you take this information and incorporate all of it into your daily living . . . its core teaching is that you know peace in your hearts, homes, and world. We are here, my friend, to bring peace to earth, to ourselves, and to others . . . whether in life or in death.

26
The Freedom Trail

Oh, Glo-bug, here we are back at your home. What a wonderful journey. That story you just shared was the exact thing I needed. I feel a sense of peace and gratitude like I never knew existed. I guess what I'm trying to say is, "I feel free" for the first time in my life. This journey has been like a roadmap for me, "The Freedom Trail," because that's what others and myself achieve after such a journey. I know I haven't added much conversation during this journey, but selfishly, I didn't feel as if I could add anything to your life. Your loved ones are right—it would be difficult to give you anything you don't already have. You do have it all.

You silly rabbit. Don't you understand that *your presence* is the gift to me? Having a gift or awareness is useless if we can't share, and give it. I needed you as much as you needed me.

What parting words would you want to give me, Doc? You've already given me a complete prescription for a

happy and fulfilled life, on every level of my being, but what is it inside you that you would still like to share?

My devotion to God would make you barf if you could hear my moment-to-moment thoughts. I am in constant communion with God every minute of every day. You can be, too. To those who are yet to understand the Presence and Power within themselves, this moment-to-moment prayer and ongoing conversation with God is incomprehensible. Once you touch the spiritual realm, the earthly, material world has less meaning. I have felt perfect love and peace and know the results.

A man in a workshop agreed to sit in my healing chair as I demonstrated before a workshop. I teach the technique, so each healer and healee is given the ability to see and feel both experiences; therefore, I repeat the teaching twice. The man was my guinea pig so that I could show the hand placements, and as I finished the second version of the same hand placements, he was overflowing with love.

He jumped out of the chair and grabbed a woman in the front row and said, "I've got so much love to give . . . I have to have a hug." As they released from the embrace, he started to walk away and very animatedly he cried out, "I still have so much love to give, let me give you another hug."

Wouldn't it be a wonderful place to live . . . if you had so much love, you had to give it away? *(Heavy sigh)* . . . I not only believe it's possible—I believe it will soon become a reality.

So many people fear if they "find God," they will become boring individuals, too holy, or without their individual personality. Nikki feared this as we began a friendship and soon discovered she would retain her individuality. You've seen that I'm about as "down-home and natural" as they come. You give up nothing to have a personal relationship with God. Some of the "things" you do may change, but without human effort. You just keep being you—and the rest will take care of itself.

When our daughter Kerrie was attending Purdue, she took a semester break and was working in Hartford, Connecticut. Kirk and I joined her for four days to give her a "family fix."

While touring the eastern states, we found ourselves in downtown Boston, walking the famous "Freedom Trail." We ended up back at the pier, where we would catch a boat to take us back to where we started.

Kirk and Kerrie were walking arm in arm ahead of me. I was lollygagging behind, taking in the sights and sounds. In my left peripheral vision, I noticed two boys running across the grass. My first thought was, "Oh, they're brothers. They're playing." However, as I turned to view the scene head on, as an observer, I realized: they aren't brothers and they definitely aren't playing.

I continued watching as the second teen caught up to the first, grabbing him and throwing him to the grass. I witnessed the aggressor punching the boy and then he began kicking him in the ribs, while he was down. Angrily, and with great strength, the first young man began kicking the boy in the head. I watched as the transgressor kicked the teen in the right temple, and my right temple exploded with pain.

At that moment, I began walking toward the fight as if they were my children. A bold, authoritative tone came from my throat as I yelled, "Hey! Knock it off!" A man, to my left, heard my cry and turned to view the situation. Quickly, he ran to the boys and broke up the fight.

I stood firmly until I saw the fight was dissolved and ran

to catch up with Kerrie and Kirk who had been unaware of the situation. Kirk had heard my end display of yelling for the boys to stop fighting and as I approached him, he was shaking his head in disbelief.

"And, Gloria," he said in a confused tone, "What were you thinking of . . . approaching a fight in a large city?" Teasing, he asked, "What? Did you think you'd karate kick him in the back of the knee?"

"Kirk, I honestly didn't think about it, but I felt no fear. It wasn't 'me' who yelled those words."

When we arrived back at the car, I sat silently in the backseat. Kirk looked into the rearview mirror and asked if I was sleeping. I wasn't sleeping. I could feel the boy's pain in my right temple and was working on him, long-distance. Being kicked in the temple could have killed that boy.

In the silence, I was also reviewing how I had just walked without fear. The old Gloria would have been frightened if she had come upon even a verbal confrontation. Never, never, never would she approach a physical display of violence.

The experience was showing me where my level of consciousness now was.

My parents were able recently to watch me in action, teaching a workshop. My mom was impressed, "Gloria, you are absolutely wonderful. An eloquent and dynamic speaker. What surprises me the most is that when you were little, we had to drag you out on stage to perform. I guess it helps because you know your subject matter so well."

Brother. Do I know my subject matter well. IT'S MY LIFE. Gloria isn't the eloquent speaker, God Is. Going before a group of people, not knowing what's going to fall out of my mouth is the most uncomfortable thing I'm asked to do. Before I approach the stage, I silently realize, "God is the teacher, and the students, including me, have appeared."

You remain so humble through all of this, Gloria. You are such an inspiration.

Thank you. As you continue to listen, you'll understand why.

When I taught in Rhode Island, following the workshop, my hostess took me down to Providence River, which runs through the town. Music played as the tourists walked along the river, which had been designed as what they called "Fire Water." Huge bonfires, blazing and beautiful, were displayed in the middle of the river. You could rent paddleboats or take gondola rides under the starry sky. It was a beautiful evening.

When I arrived in Rhode Island, my Japanese hostess said that the thing she wanted most to learn from me was how to become comfortable expressing thoughts and feelings. Her culture had not allowed this and she wanted to at least be able to share how she felt with her children.

As we walked along the river, I noticed a boatload of people passing by and "none of them were in their bodies," enjoying the moment. You could tell they were daydreaming and missing the experience. I leaned over the rail and raised my voice, "Wow. I'll bet you're all having a wonderful time."

The people in the boat "came back into present moment," looked up to me with smiles and affirmed, "Yes, this is fun—we're having a wonderful time."

My hostess was shocked. "Gloria. I can't believe you just did that."

"What?" I asked. "The people weren't enjoying their experience. I just brought them awareness of how special what they're doing is."

My hostess still couldn't believe I'd just done that (and good grief—in public, with so many people around). She had taken it personally. Her culture of judgments and fears created embarrassment. (You'll soon see that "I have one mean gene.")

"Those people are never going to see me again—but even if they did, I didn't do anything wrong. I wasn't bad."

Again, my hostess said, "Well, I'm embarrassed and I can't believe you did that."

"That embarrassed you? Then . . . watch this."

Once again I leaned over and raised my voice as a gondola boat was being paddled past us with a man and woman sitting cozily and romantically side by side. I said to the woman, "I hope that man is whispering in your ear how beautiful you look tonight in the moonlight," and she smiled and nodded that he was. . . .

My hostess barked, "That's it! We're going home."

At 2:00 A.M., she and I were still talking when she asked, "Who are you?" Thinking senility had set in early on her, I replied, "I am Gloria D. Benish . . . you flew me here to teach a workshop."

She laughed and said, "No. I keep seeing faces superimpose themselves over yours. First, Jesus, then Mother Mary, then angels . . . then other faces. Who are you?"

Teasingly, I repeated, "I'm Gloria D. Benish . . . you flew me here to teach a workshop."

Still shaking her head, she said, "When you were teaching the workshop, me and the lady sitting next to me kept poking each other, whispering *"Are you seeing what I'm seeing?"* She said, "Gloria, during the workshop, your skin and bones became translucent and it was as if God was standing before the audience, teaching us directly."

He was.

Glo-bug, you live such a full life, and I'm sure that everything you do is fun, but what are your outlets for re-

laxation? Do you ever just go away from the world and their needs and relax?

I love the ocean and dream of having a home one day on the cliffside and listening to the heartbeat of the ocean as I continue to write inspirational books. Also, Kirk and I recently bought a long-awaited pop-up camper. His love for the woods didn't quite match my idea of camping in my parent's thirty-foot motor home with the bathroom, the color TV, and the VCR, as well as the popping corn they store in what we teasingly call their $200 bread box. He and I compromised and purchased the camper and go for weekend get-aways.

One of those outings was outside Spokane, Washington, with other family members.

Have you ever experienced a "Musical Rainstick?" My first encounter was in the Salt Lake City airport while browsing through one of the gift shops during a layover in my travels. They come in all sizes and I chose one for each of my family members as well as my friend Nikki. The rainsticks are musical and ceremonial, used by various groups from ancient times to present day. Their soothing and soul-reaching rainlike sound is produced when held by either end of the rainstick, allowing small pebbles inside to trickle down through sharp thorns that have been pounded into the interior of the stick in a spiral formation.

The rainstick sound is very relaxing, peaceful, and nurturing. They assist in self-realization and improvement, stress reduction, and health improvement. For many people, they are a toy or conversation piece; however, my intent in sharing this information is to make your life more peaceful, relaxed, and comfortable.

Back to the recent camp-out. During the first day, the clouds gathered and it forced everyone back into their campers. I attempted to read a book, at random, but felt more called to renew my Spirit in the Light. As I closed my eyes and opened myself to the Presence of God, I felt uplifted. I felt as if I had become a rainstick. The sound of the water upon the roof was pleasant and enjoyable, calming and serene beyond anything I had experienced in a long time due to my hectic life and schedule. I never wanted the moment to end. I felt strengthened and warm amidst the soggy and clammy, cold environment.

Following the rainstorm, I walked the trail with my sister-in-law, Debbie, and hundreds of butterflies went before us. I watched as the beautiful red, orange, yellow, gold, peacock-colored, purple, and white butterflies flitted to and fro. There were so many, it was as if we were in a kaleidoscope of them. It was good that we were taking small and easy steps, because they settled on the ground before our steps and teased us, as if they were going to sit upon our shoes and hitchhike to the next stop.

They almost threatened to sit upon my shoulder and dared to look me directly in the eyes and tell me that I was trusted. I continued to look upon their beauty with such knowingness that great transformation was forthcoming.

A bluebird also flew directly toward me as if it were going to sit upon my shoulder, and the courage it exhibited shocked me as my "Oh wow" startled it, in return. I knew how St. Francis must have felt as all creatures, great and small, felt his peace. I felt a lily pad for the first time that weekend and was surprised that it was a living, growing part of the lake and not just a leaf that floated on the water. The innocence of that, and floating upon the water, paddling my first canoe . . . and enjoying the baby beaver . . . what a beautiful weekend was given to me in the silence and beauty of the forest. I felt so free, the way you're feeling today.

We're all seeking freedom, and don't forget little Scott's reply to me when he was sharing his "Comet" advice. If I would continue doing this daily, I would receive a reward: freedom.

Freedom from fear, doubt, and the beliefs of dual powers is the greatest achievement a soul will attain in this dimension. In order to walk, as a master without fear, we must surrender each judgment of duality. When I meet an "appearance" of a disease or situation and I'm not feeling confident to be used by Spirit effectively, I get about as real as one can get in order to humble myself. "God, I don't know what in the hell I'm doing, so I give thanks and trust that You do."

If the "appearance continues to frighten me," I might say, "Ya know, God, with the judgments I have (concerning that which I'm looking upon), plus my programming from parents, society, and friends, I feel I have a limited understanding to deal with this in a spiritual sense. I'm not inviting You into the physical world—I am asking You to raise my consciousness, of this situation, to a spiritual level so that I can see this "thing" the way You would. I'm asking that my tunnel vision of this situation be healed and restored . . . asking You to interpret this Divine Idea for me. I give thanks, for it is already done."

The above ideas can help you meet those situations that frighten or overwhelm you, or the events that you find difficult.

I walked the Freedom Trail that our forefathers walked. It was a direct manifestation of my state of consciousness. (Remember that everything we need is already embodied within our consciousness.) As you continue to open yourself daily to the Presence, situations you no longer choose to experience in your life will fade. As we each can look upon experiences of the human scene, without judgment, we'll walk together on the Freedom Trail.

It's time, I guess, for our journey to come to a close. I appreciate my family's support, allowing me this get-away with you. I'm going to miss you, Gloria. I have that lovely warm glow filling and surrounding me again. My soul feels renewed, my spirit is healed, and I passionately and lovingly am willing for all that awaits me.

I've certainly enjoyed this time we have had together and I'll look forward to hearing from you. Until then, I'm off to create some new experiences and express more love, so no matter how many books I write or you read, you'll hear new and exciting adventures and receive understanding that you can incorporate in your life. So, my precious, until we can meet again, give me a hug . . .

Glo-bug, you are such a blessing. I love you with my whole, great big heart—and I ain't kidding either. Whenever I feel fear, I'm going to close my eyes, look to the Light, and remember this hug. Safe in your arms, I can feel your gentleness and loving strength.

Thanks. I'm not letting go until you tell me. . . .

Take care, I care . . .
From my heart and home,
Gloria

Epilogue

(I'LL NEVER GIVE UP, NEVER GIVE UP, NEVER GIVE UP)

Several times throughout the year, I cook our family a turkey dinner with all the trimmings. I don't wait until November to give my gratitude for all that we, as a family, have to be grateful for. Last year as I was preparing one of these meals, I'd had a very busy day doing private healings for out-of-town guests. I had just enough time to jump in the shower and with wet, flat hair, I went to the sink to peel potatoes for the evening banquet.

Danielle walked into the kitchen and as I glanced at her, I could feel something was wrong. I asked if she was okay and she responded, "No, Mom, I'm about to start crying . . . I need a hug."

Her now tall, five-foot-seven frame fell heavily into my arms, leaning on me as she sobbed. I asked what was wrong and her thoughts and feelings poured from her lips, through sobbing. As you read these words, please think how it would sound as it came from her open heart, taking tremendous energy to get each word past the tears.

"I'm reading *Go Within or Go Without* and I'm so proud

of you, Mom." Startled, because the book had been off the press for years, I asked if she was just now reading it for the first time.

"Yes . . . and I'm so proud of you."

I asked what she was proud of and she replied, "Everything!" I teased, to lighten the mood and said, "Danielle, *everything* doesn't make a very good book report."

I asked why she was crying and she replied, "I started crying in the introduction and have cried ever since because I'm so proud of you." She swallowed hard before she said, "And you just can't ever stop doing it." I assured her I wasn't going to. She went on to explain that I affected people's lives and twice more repeated, "You just can't *ever* stop doing this, Mom. People need you!"

I asked, while still holding her, "Why are you saying that I can't give up? Where did you ever get the idea I would stop?" Swallowing hard again, she replied, "I heard you talking to Dad and you told him that you can't imagine sitting here for the rest of your life, answering that telephone."

I laughed. "Danielle, you didn't hear the entire conversation. Dad and I have just been discussing how I can effectively reach more people. Either I . . . or trained receptionists will always be here to receive calls from people in need."

Danielle continued to share her teenage viewpoint of the service I perform. "People who have never felt loved before . . . do . . . after they've read your book, heard you speak, or felt your arms around them." I was truly touched that Danielle understood the service I have chosen for God and humanity in this life.

I asked, during the hug and through her tears, "Danielle, wasn't it you—about a month ago—who was so angry that you had ever taught me how to heal by giving others a little extra love?"

She whispered "Yes."

"Weren't you just bitching at me, that if you had never taught me how to do this, I would be a normal mom like other kids have . . . and I'd be home on weekends with you?"

She whispered a second "Yes."

"But, I was wrong, Mom. People need you."

I said, "Danielle, you have to let me go—I need to get these potatoes peeled so that I can get dinner on" and she cried louder, "Dinner can wait—I still need to hug!"

I don't know when I've been as proud of Danielle as I was during the fifteen-minute embrace. If my youngest teenager "got it," then I trust humanity will, as well.

No, Danielle. No, world. I'll never give up, never give up, never give up.

Other Books by Gloria D. Benish

Available at your local bookstore or from Citadel Press:

> *Go Within or Go Without*
> *(A simple guide to self-healing)*
> ISBN #0-8065-2256-9

Available through: www.miraclehealing.org

> *As God Is My Witness*
> ISBN #0-9636100-0-7

> *To Become As Little Children*
> *(Fairy tales for adults . . .)*
> ISBN #0-9636100-1-5

About the Author

GLORIA D. BENISH is one of today's fastest rising inspirational authors. Her works include those of self-help and personal growth, dealing with many of today's sensitive issues. She guides the readers to look within for the answers, and leaves one and all with the feeling of love for today, and hope for tomorrow.

A wife and a mother to four children, she opens her heart to reach all those in need. Gloria lives in Montana.